TAPESTRY

A City Girl, a Country Boy, and the Master Weaver

Judy Scofield

The author has changed some names in this book to protect the privacy of certain individuals. Names in quotes are pseudonyms.

Editor: JW Editing

Cover Design: Logan Runyon

Cover Tapestry: Belonging to Olga Schultz (Judy's Grandmother)

CONTENTS

DEDICATION
To the Giants of the Faith

Don Gast and Bill Wurzel – God brought them into our lives in the birthing of Five Pines Ministries, and God continued to use them in a mighty way – Don for over thirty-five years and Bill for thirty years. Indeed they were the "Golden Threads" of the entire Tapestry.

Our First Board Members – They were willing to join Jim and step out in faith and trust God for a new ministry without any programming or buildings established.

Harv Chrouser – He was a visionary in Christian camping and a visionary in the inception of Five Pines. He was a "Golden Thread" as well.

Our Family – They believed in and supported Jim in releasing the historical family farm into the Lord's hands and trusting God to use it to bring glory to Him.

Life-long Supporters – Their faithfulness, never failing. Many have supported the ministry from its early beginnings.

Jim Wing – He was the first person to take the step (besides us) and trust the Lord to come on as a full-time staff member at Five Pines. He was on staff from 1991 – 2006. Pastor Wing's first love and true faithfulness was to the Word of God.

FROM THE FOUNDER

The Power of God:
Interwoven in Creating the Ministry of Five Pines

"Great is the Lord and most worthy of praise; His greatness no one can fathom. One generation will commend your works to another; they will tell of your mighty acts." – Psalm 145:3-4

FOR OVER ONE HUNDRED YEARS, my father and forefathers cultivated these forty acres of land, harvesting fruit and vegetables on what was known as Five Pines Farm. They meticulously planted the seeds anticipating a great harvest. Now God is using this same land to cultivate hearts, to plant seeds, and harvest souls for His Kingdom.

For thirty-five years Judy and I have experienced an awesome work of His hands as He and He alone would weave people, ideas, materials and finances together to establish the beautiful Tapestry of what is now Five Pines Ministries. Since 1979, God has used hundreds of people to accomplish this harvest. It has indeed been a privilege to witness God's power in our lives, and we do not take that lightly.

God gave us the desire, and He provided the tools to bring young people to the love and knowledge of Jesus Christ our Savior. My prayer is that God would continue to use His Word, His people, this land, and these facilities to convey His principles to change lives.

Jim Scofield, Founder and Past Director

PREFACE

IN DECEMBER OF 1979, I found myself standing in the middle of an old school bus that had been converted into a camping van. My husband Jim had bought the converted bus (probably built for the former owner's northern Michigan hunting trips), thinking it would be perfect for his future wilderness trip plans with local teens.

I, Judy Scofield, was a 39-year-old mother of two young teens, and two very overprotective parents had raised me in the city. Now I found myself headed to Florida, not to lie on the beach in sunny Naples, but to our final destination of a southernmost beach in the Everglades – to canoe and camp!

I watched out the back window as I nervously gripped one of the back seats on the bus. It was the rickety old canoe trailer that captivated my attention. The old trailer seemed to bounce all over the road with its five canoes strapped down. I had to pinch myself and think about what a crazy thing we were doing. Jim was excited to lead a group of thirteen people, mostly teenagers, on this southern-bound trip. We were gone for thirteen days over Christmas break to, of all things, canoe through the Everglades to the very tip of Florida and out to the gulf coast to camp for a few days.

My mind played over and over the cautious advice of my father's voice: *"Never get into a canoe because they are so unstable."* I wondered what we were getting ourselves into. What type of adventure did God have in store for us? In my mind, the Everglades were notorious for things like poisonous snakes, alligators, and a massive mosquito population. I prayed, "Lord, give me a calm heart, a love for these kids, and a trust in my husband's adventurous plans. Lead, protect, and provide."

Little did I know that this was only the beginning of the adventures God had in store for Jim and Judy Scofield. We were on our way to one of the most memorable experiences of my life; but it was only the beginning of thirty-five years of watching God work, not only in our lives, but also in the lives of hundreds of children and teens.

I would be challenged to walk with the Lord and follow my loving husband – and experience God in ways I never dreamed of. Only God could have allowed us the privilege of living the lives we have led. As we now enter into semi-retirement, we know the stories must be told for future generations.

Tapestry is the history of our walk with God, His leading and providing for a small Christian camp nestled back on a dirt road in Berrien Center, Michigan. It is the story of a loving God who took two people who were spiritually blind, a 150-year-old collapsing barn, and thirty-three acres of an overgrown farm to create a camp where people would be challenged and blessed to hear and experience the love of God in their lives. It is about the power of God's awesome works and proclaiming His great deeds.

The following quote from Billy Graham so fits the thoughts and experiences of this book:

"Those who submit to the will of God do not fight back at life. They learn the secret of yielding – of relinquishing and abandoning – their own lives and wills to Christ. And then He gives back to them a life that is far richer and fuller than anything they could ever have imagined."

INTRODUCTION
"The Story"

"If anyone would come after me, he must deny himself and take up his cross and follow me." – Matthew 16:24

IT WAS THE FALL OF 2007. Jim and I were waiting to greet a busload of middle school students. They were from a church in Itasca, Illinois, and their pastors were taking them on a confirmation retreat. They had been holding their church/school confirmation retreat in the Carriage House Lodge at Five Pines Ministries every two years since 2001.

As was usually the case in hosting retreats, we would welcome the group to Five Pines in the Carriage House Lodge and briefly cover some rules. Then if the timing seemed appropriate, we would give a brief history and testimony of God's work so that the group had some idea where they were at and why the ministry was called Five Pines.

As the group of students got off the bus and unloaded all their gear, one of the pastors asked us if there was anything we wanted to speak to the students about. We just shared a brief welcome, thinking we could speak to them more the next day. The group had ordered pizza and was anxious to head over to the Activity Center for an informal evening of games and food.

Jim and I got on our golf cart and drove over to the Activity Center to make sure the lights were on and the tables were set with chairs. It was a beautiful autumn evening, and we sat in front of the Activity Center admiring the clear night sky and enjoying the crisp fresh air.

Soon the group of students walked over to the Activity Center with their two pastors. One of the pastors came over to us and said, "You didn't tell them The Story."

At first we didn't know what he meant. Then we realized and replied, "We don't always tell *The Story*, especially if the group is a returning group and may have heard it before."

He said, "Oh no, I think it is important that these kids hear The Story. Come on in, and I'll introduce you to my students – and *please* tell them."

The Story has been repeated literally hundreds of times to individuals just touring the ministry grounds, parents of campers, guest groups whom we have hosted on weekend retreats in the lodge, seminars we were asked to facilitate at Christian camping conferences, and area churches interested in Five Pines.

Tapestry is The Story. It is about the desire God laid on our hearts to simply let go and let Him fulfill the purpose He had planned for us. It is the history of all the miracles He has done over the past thirty-five years. It is also a story to be shared with others who might feel the Divine tug at their hearts to step out into an unknown area and trust God fully.

Tapestry is not about Jim and Judy Scofield. It is about God creating a ministry to reach out and touch the lives in their local community and beyond with the message of Christ's redemption for a sinful world. It is a story expressing the ongoing work God has done and desires to do in every believer's life. It is our desire, as the apostle Paul stated, *"that you and I may be mutually encouraged by each other's faith"* (Romans 1:12).

We have tried to create in this book a pictorial weaving of how God used both the dark and light experiences in our lives. It is how He added textures into the experiences by intricately weaving both easy and difficult challenges throughout the *Tapestry*. It is a beautiful picture of how God brought people into our lives; sometimes for a short period, others being woven in and out as the ministry progressed, and others for a longer duration. Each person accomplished God's purpose to help create a rich, complex design of His choosing: *The Tapestry of Five Pines Ministries.*

ONE

Early Weavings: A City Girl, a Country Boy, and Jesus

"For I know the plans I have for you,' declares the Lord ..." – Jeremiah 29:11

EACH OF US HAS A HISTORY. Our early years have a significant purpose in forming who we are and why we act as we do. Those early years, our roles in our families, and how we were programmed to respond to life, bring us into adulthood sometimes with many questions. We believe that only God can take both the negative and the positive in our lives and use them to His glory (which we believe is the ultimate purpose of life).

Psalm 139 speaks so beautifully of how well God knows us: *He created us and His works are wonderful. He knows our innermost thoughts and our days He has numbered.* I did not have the privilege of learning those precious truths until adulthood and have often thought, *"Would my striving to achieve to be somebody been different had I known Jesus Christ as my Lord in my youth?"*

My dear mother, Valentina (Schultz) Rose, was born in Ukraine, Russia of German ancestry in 1915. At the turn of the century, nearly 200,000 German families had migrated to an area between Poland and Ukraine, Russia. Entire farming communities were of the Lutheran faith and were centered in Volhynia, a gubernia (province) of the Russian Empire.

In 1914, one year before my mother was born, Germany declared war on Russia, and the Russians became more hostile to the German colonists. Many of their lands were confiscated by the Russians. Some German colonists served in the Russian Army. The Russians were concerned that these soldiers of German descent would turn on them.

Nearly 100,000 German colonists were deported to Siberia, and many of them perished not long after. Alex Schultz and his young family were basically living in "ground zero" of one huge conflict after another. The revolution became widespread over Russia, and thousands of people were affected. My grandfather was quite prominent in his small town. Grandpa Alex owned a butcher shop with a specialty in making sausage.

When the Czarist government collapsed, the Bolsheviks became the strongest political power. They believed that the government owned everything, even small businesses such as Grandpa Alex's butcher shop. The story we have been told over the years (and we cannot document) is that the Bolshevik army stormed through his small town, producing terror in the hearts of each citizen. The raging Bolshevik army took Grandpa Alex and confiscated his shop.

Later Alex was released and reunited with his wife and family. In 1920, Alex, Olga, and their two small children, Paul and Valentina, fled to Bromberg, Poland. They then boarded *The Carolina* in London, England, destined for freedom in the United States of America. Paul was nine and Valentina was five at this tumultuous time. I feel Grandpa and his family were saved for such a time as this!

After the long difficult journey across a turbulent ocean, the sight of the Statue of Liberty filled Alex and Olga and their children with hearts of hope and anticipation. It was November 21, 1920 when they disembarked their ship at the infamous and dismal Ellis Island – Alex clutching just eighty cents in his pockets.

After three days of the delousing procedure and filling out all the paperwork, relatives who were their sponsors met them and escorted them to the state of Michigan to begin a new life! Alex and Olga were members of the Lutheran Church, and God eventually led them to a community of fellow German believers in St. Joseph, Michigan.

For this young couple, it was indeed a comfort to be among people who shared their courage and great expectations in a new land of freedom; who not only spoke their language but also were of the same faith and had similar experiences. Inhabitants in this small community of German immigrants were known as "sand rabbits" because they lived below the bluff in St. Joseph on the shores of Lake Michigan. Alex and Olga didn't speak the language and Alex needed a job, but soon this small family settled in with other relatives and began a new life in America.

My mother, Valentina, was a sweet and loving little girl who drew much attention with her "curtsies" and "dunka" ("thank you" in German) to anyone who showed her attention. She was a beautiful little girl and was asked to be the flower girl for a variety of weddings. Some of the couples she didn't even know.

Valentina's early childhood had a deep impact on her adult life. I believe she always struggled to be accepted and feel self-worth. Even when she became engaged to my father, Lawrence Rose, his family did not want to accept someone from the "sand rabbit" community. Mom had to prove herself worthy of their acceptance. This was passed down and lived out in her adult life as a mother and wife as well. Low self-esteem is not uncommon in immigrant populations and has often been part of the "baggage" that immigrants carry as they transition from the Bolshevik oppression to America, a land of accomplishment and wealth.

Mom had a great heart and generous spirit. I believe she believed in God but didn't understand a personal relationship with Christ until her later years. She was a wonderful cook, very creative at sewing, and always had busy hands crocheting things and giving them away. My talented and thrifty mother sewed all of the clothes her three daughters wore. She savored much pride in her handiwork and in her cooking.

There was a lot of love in my family, and we often had other families over for a meal. "Tiny", as she was called, became very well known for her delicious meals. My Dad was also blessed with the gracious gift of hospitality. People loved to come to the Roses' for dinner – it was a happy household.

We were not a family of means, but had a wonderful life together. My father worked in a factory but gave generously to friends and family. Dad and Mom loved each other and showed their affection for each other constantly. Daddy "babied" his three daughters and openly showed his affection for us as well. He also saw himself as the chief worrier and protector for us all.

I believe Mom found satisfaction and self-worth in a performance-driven life. She thrived on her accomplishments. In a very direct way it was passed on to me as I grew up. I was the oldest of three girls and I, in turn; felt I had to always perform so Mom could be proud of my accomplishments. She sacrificed much for her family and was very proud of everything we did. Sometimes I became very prideful of my accomplishments because of my strong will and perfectionist approach to life. God used this strong "will to achieve" to show me the sin of pride.

Later, as a Christian, I would learn that a performance-driven life is not of God. Just as the Apostle Paul said, *"Am I now trying to win the approval of men, or of God? Or am I trying to please men? If I were still trying to please men, I would not be a servant of Christ"* (Galatians 1:10). I discovered what it meant to be a servant of Christ – to let go and let God be the Lord of my life. At this time in my life, though, I could *never* have understood what the following Scripture meant:

"Love not the world, neither the things that are in the world. If any man love the world, the love of the Father is not in him. For all that is in the world, the lust of the flesh, the lust of the eyes and the PRIDE OF LIFE, is not of the Father, but is of the world. And the world passeth away, and the lust thereof: but he that doeth the will of God abideth forever" (1 John 2:15-17 KJV, emphasis mine).

God has often used failure to bring a person to their knees and realize that the pride they had in their accomplishments was a sin. Never in a million years would I have put pride in the same category as the awful sins of "lust of the flesh" and "lust of the eyes", but there it was in 1 John 2:16: "the pride of life". The "lusts" were without a doubt sins, but pride?!! I was raised to believe that it was important to be proud of what one had accomplished.

֍ ֍ ֍ ֍ ֍ ֍ ֍

The Man of My Life:
A Country Boy – A Contrasting Thread
"A patient man has great understanding." – Proverbs 14:29a

At age sixteen, I fell deeply in love with Jim Scofield, the man of my life. Jim was two years older than I was, very gentle and easygoing. His early life was the exact opposite of mine. He was raised as an only child to older parents in a simple life on a farm called Five Pines Farm. From early on in our dating relationship, I knew in my heart we would marry. I loved his easy way of life, especially his gentleness, his purity of life, and the joy he brought to my heart. Life was very simple to him and so refreshing to me. I was a city girl, and Jim was a farm boy with a very profound lineage. Opposites do attract!

Jim's ancestry can be traced back to the sixteenth century on both of his parent's sides. Many of his relatives came from England and were very early settlers in America. John *"Mayflower Compact"* Alden is Jim's ninth great grandfather removed. History states he was first "to leap" on Plymouth Rock. The delightful Longfellow poem, *The Courtship of Miles Standish*, has given John Alden and his bride Priscilla Mullens worldwide celebrity status, though it is feared its historical accuracy would hardly stand up to criticism.

Unlike my ancestors, whose hardships came when they relocated from Germany to America in the 1920's, Jim's family members lived through the unbelievable hardships of the pioneering life of early America during the 1600's and 1700's. Baldwin Jenkins (Jim's third great grandfather) was born in Pennsylvania in 1783. In 1824, when he was living in Ohio, he persuaded a number of families to join him in moving to Michigan. They came as far as Fort Wayne and all but Baldwin got discouraged and returned to Ohio.

Baldwin continued alone to trek the one hundred miles from Fort Wayne to the banks of the St. Joseph River. He picked out a spot to his liking (among many fruit trees) called Pokagon Prairie. He returned to Ohio, told of his fruitful discovery, and then returned to Michigan in the spring to raise a crop of corn.

In the fall he came back to Ohio to get his wife, Mary, and their five children. *Not wanting to put extra weight on the wagon, the Jenkins family walked all the way from Ohio to the Pokagon area!* They finally arrived in Michigan in November, exhausted but excited about their new home.

The first winter they lived in a wigwam on a dirt floor – corn, maize, and meat being their only food. Baldwin transported their harvested corn eight miles for grinding at a nearby mill in Niles in order to make their bread. Their first winter in 1826 was severe and the snow was so very deep. They had to brave the brutal weather to lift up the cattle's feet, rub them with a handful of straw, and then drive them around to keep them from lying on the ground and freezing to death.

The second of their six children, Eliza, was born in Ohio in 1815 before they traveled to Michigan. At nineteen, she married Isaac Murphy and they lived all of their nearly sixty years of married life raising *thirteen* children in Berrien Center, Michigan.

Eliza, Jim's great, great grandmother, was a writer extraordinaire, recording volumes of memoirs of her life. Her writings, all in prose, revealed pages and pages of the hardships and joys of her pioneer life in Berrien Township. She died just five days after her husband's death in 1893.

Here's a comment from her obituary: *"Mrs. Murphy was a woman of strong faith in Christ and efficacy of prayer, and when her husband was taken away she earnestly desired to depart and be with him in a better world. It may be said of Mr. & Mrs. Murphy: 'They were lovely and pleasant in their lives, and in death they were not divided.'"*

ౠ ౠ ౠ ౠ ౠ ౠ ౠ

Five Pines Farm: A Major Thread Woven

Two of Isaac and Eliza's thirteen children, John Murphy (born 1841) and Albert Murphy (born 1845), are both in a direct line as Jim's great grandfathers. This is a very important fact in Jim's long line of ancestors. John's son, Miles, and Albert's daughter, Cora, were first cousins. They were married and were Jim's grandparents. Miles and Cora lived with Jim and his parents in the home at Five Pines Farm during the 1930's and 40's when Jim was just a child.

Jim's family farm came into his family through his great grandfather John Murphy's wife, Annette Snow. Her father, Orin D. Snow, came from Milton, Vermont to homestead the original forty-acre farm in 1839. Orin was a millwright and cabinet-maker who built many gristmills in the Southwestern Michigan area. In 1845, he built the Vermont Colonial style house we still live in today. He also planted the five white pine trees in the front yard. (Only four of the original five remain today)

In the 1800's most roads weren't named and there certainly wasn't any postal service. All farms were known by their names, and thus the farm with the beautiful Vermont structured home was known as Five Pines Farm.

སྙ སྙ སྙ སྙ སྙ སྙ སྙ

Grandpa Albert's Legacy

Jim's Great Grandpa Albert's life is also a very important thread woven into the *Tapestry* story. Not only was he an author of volumes of historical poetry, but he also was a deeply convicted believer. His most valued masterpiece is his seven-page testimony of his conversion from being an "infidel" to a follower of Jesus Christ.

Albert rejected Christianity through his young adult life. He had a strong desire to find Scripture that contradicted itself and a driving ambition to become rich. However, in February 1876 at the age of thirty-one, he experienced a strong conviction to humble himself and answer the call to become a follower of Christ. His wife, Sarah Jane, was not ready and at first rejected a walk with the Lord. But one night about 11:00 p.m., Albert and his wife pledged to each other to begin to serve the Lord. In his own words:

"I would pledge in my heart that at some time I would go to the full extent of my ability to so submit my will to the will of a just Creator as to free myself of all moral responsibility and fear of the future."

Albert was concerned about what this meant. Would he be willing to totally let go of everything: friends, family and all his property? This was painful. It was like signing his own death warrant, but he consented. He even traveled by horseback, to every person he knew, and some he didn't know, about their need to confess their sins and accept Christ's forgiveness. He went on to preach and speak all over the country and be a part of the great revivals of 1875-76. Little did Jim and I know that one hundred years later another significant surrender to the Lord would happen.

TWO

Contrasting Threads Entwined As One
"And the Lord God said It is not good that man should be alone" Genesis 2:18

WHEN I BEGAN DATING JIM, I felt somewhat confused. What was a Christian? I always thought we were Christians because we went to church. Many students who transferred from the parochial school I had attended to the public high school did not act like Christians. Once they were in public school, they changed their values immensely – especially the athletes. In my high school many of the athletes smoked and drank to be "cool".

On the other hand, Jim lettered in four sports during his high school years but was as "clean-cut" as they come. I believe that is one reason I was drawn to him. He had no inhibitions and was always happy. Jim's parents took him to Sunday school as a child, and he played on the church softball team. Yet he didn't go to church regularly as a teen and neither did his parents. He did recall going forward at a youth conference at Gull Lake but never grew in his walk with the Lord.

We were engaged on Christmas day, 1958, and planned to be married the next February. If my father said it once he said it a thousand times: "You can't plan a wedding in a month." Jim was in the Air Force in Texas and in the process of being transferred to Columbus, Ohio. I missed him immensely and so desired to be with him. I was just nineteen and Jim was twenty-one and, as in the case of most young marriages, we probably weren't ready. We did plan everything in a month, and it was just the kind of wedding we wanted – simple and not too challenging. There was one exception: Jim's transfer to Ohio was delayed, and he barely made it home in time for the wedding. Whew! We married in the big denominational church I was raised in and currently attended.

I expected Jim to be a husband and father just like my father. I waited for him to step into those roles, but Jim's personality was not at all like my father's. My father was a perfectionist, extremely creative, and early at *everything* in his life. He was overprotective and worried beyond reason. My father would make sure the car was warmed up *a half hour* before my mother and her three girls went anywhere. My dad's theory in life was: "We had better fix the loose brick on the chimney before it falls off and hurts someone."

On the other hand, Jim's example of fatherhood was not anywhere *near* the same. Jim's father was more laid back, and his theory in life was: "If the brick doesn't fall today, it may not fall tomorrow; so why worry about it. We'll fix it when it falls."

My father lovingly bought his wife and three daughters' corsages every Easter and Mother's Day. In contrast to my father's expressions of love and generosity, Jim's father gave Jim and me money to buy his wife his very first Christmas gift to her – and she was in her eighties! The gift was a Bible. My father and mother showed affection often. I never really saw Jim's parents express their love, but we knew they loved each other.

In our early years of marriage, our expectations of wedded bliss created no more than the average conflicts for a young married couple. I can say Jim and I were very happy. I loved being a wife. We couldn't afford a honeymoon, so we immediately moved to Columbus, Ohio, near Lockbourne Air Force base. We lived there for three years and never attended church at any time. I guess we didn't feel it was important.

In 1960 our first child, Tanya, was born in Ohio during our second year of marriage. Of course, in our eyes she was close to a perfect child. My mother always wanted a red- headed, freckle-faced boy. I adamantly did not. But God blessed us with a little girl with the most beautiful, attention-getting light auburn–hair. God fulfilled my mother's desire and also *my* desire because of her beauty even as a child. Tanya wore her heart on the outside and still does to this day – a giver of love to many.

Our second child, Kirk, was an inquisitive and intelligent little blond boy. He was born during our first year out of the service. Kirk was special to me because I came from a family of all girls, and now Jim and I had both a son and a daughter – a perfect family.

During the year 1963, we experienced a lot of turmoil. We were now out of the Air Force, and we moved our mobile home back to Michigan. We set it up on Jim's family farm in Berrien Center, right behind the main house and near the backdoor of his parents.

Jim had a difficult time settling into a job when we moved back. He still saw life as simple, even though some very serious problems brought on more tension within our marriage. I needed to be forgiving and not so demanding. Marriage isn't always easy, especially when the Lord is not in it. We soon purchased a house near Benton Harbor (where Jim had a job at Whirlpool Corporation) in Fairplain, Michigan. Life got so much better.

With our latest move, I was able to open a baton twirling studio in our home. All my young life I twirled in competitions around the country – sometimes every weekend. At seventeen, I had the privilege of representing Michigan at the NBTA Nationals in Saint Paul, Minnesota, and placed fifth in the finals. My winnings brought me many trophies and much pride.

We eventually formed a large competitive traveling drum and twirling corps which consisted of students from local high schools. The corps was highly successful, and with a sponsorship we were able to travel to competitions around the state. Jim was also heavily involved, and we were definitely living a performance-driven life. We proudly displayed many large trophies in our basement studio. It is difficult to say whether it drove us or we drove ourselves, but we had a passion to achieve and it brought us much pride. We loved working with the students, but our family was in jeopardy.

Tanya was also involved in twirling competitions and had won many trophies on her own. When I took her to a doctor one day and told him she had a problem gritting her teeth, he said it was stress! Any way you look at it – great accomplishments or not – this endeavor had to go! I vowed my family would never see a baton again!

We only acknowledged God on Sundays, if we went to church at all. Even as I look back, God enabled us to do some mighty great things and blessed us immensely (things that we didn't realize God was doing). This thing called pride would eventually be used by the Lord to bring me to Himself. It was 1968, and little did we realize God was directing us into something bigger than we had ever imagined – including a deep relationship with Him.

🐿 🐿 🐿 🐿 🐿 🐿 🐿

Woven Back to Jim's Roots – Reclaiming Five Pines Farm

One winter day in 1969, we drove to the old farm and began to think that maybe moving out to the country would be great for our family. The house was cold because Jim's parents were spending the winter in Florida, but the warmth of its ancient history drew us to think maybe someday our family would call it home.

In 1970 we decided to make that move. Tanya was ten-years-old, Kirk was seven, and our destination was to the historic homestead of Jim's family: Five Pines Farm. We moved from a small suburban home in Fairplain to the large but rundown Vermont-style country home with thirty-seven acres of farmland. Jim grew up on the farm, and his parents were unable to keep the house up as they grew older. They were willing to move into a mobile home directly behind the house and let us move into the original house.

It was a great place to raise our children, but the 150-year-old house needed a massive remodeling job. The barn was literally falling down, and the land hadn't been farmed in over twenty years. The wooded acreage was overrun with vines and berry bushes, and the open fields had become weed lots. But we were ambitious and adventurous. We began remodeling the house: a new heating system, insulation, a new foundation, a new roof, removing all the horsehair plaster on the inside walls, taking out walls and re-siding the outside.

The first summer we worked hard replacing 120 windowpanes and re-puttying over 300 panes before we ever moved in. But great things were happening to O.D. Snow's original creation. Rooms became much larger, two bedrooms on the main level became a new kitchen and dining room, and the beautiful main staircase was finally exposed in the living room for everyone to enjoy. The original kitchen became a family room. The front door, which hadn't been used for years because of the settling of the foundation, now easily opened. It took us nearly ten years of hard work to see the fruits of our labor – a beautiful home. Jim's mother would walk through the house and say "I wonder what Grandpa Snow would say?" For the most part she approved.

Tanya and Kirk enjoyed exploring all the acreage and we soon purchased two ponies for them. Tanya got the first pony, Little Red, for her eleventh birthday, and at the time we didn't realize he was trained to compete in contesting (barrel racing). Tanya soon learned Little Red was very stubborn and loved to run. Whenever he got out, I knew he was running to Dowagiac because he could run so fast.

Kirk's black Welsh pony, Fanny, came within the next year, and she loved to pull the two-wheel cart that she was trained on. Fanny proved to be an outstanding trail horse and brought awards to Kirk in trail horsemanship at the Fair. Fanny, though, had a temper and would take off and run wherever she wanted. Once she ran and jumped up on the front porch with Kirk on her back. She was also notorious for stepping through the barbed wire fence, crossing the road to enter an orchard to munch on a few delicious apples.

Years later, we built a new pole barn and moved the horses out of the original 1850 barn. Fanny would hit the light switch with her nose and turn the lights on. Night after night we'd go to bed and soon the outside barn light was on. We always figured someone forgot to turn it off, but then we realized that it came on in the middle of the night. Here was the main clue to the mystery: The light switch was just above the door to the grain bin. Guess who was trying to get in the grain bin and hit the switch with her nose? We loved those two little ponies, and it was a great experience for our children.

Eventually we were able to buy two full-size horses: an appaloosa named Troubles for Kirk and a beautiful black thoroughbred named Hodge Podge for Tanya. Kirk wanted a horse that was not broken so that he could train him, and Troubles was his challenge. As soon as he trained Troubles to ride, he wanted to sell him and move on to another challenge – like the nighttime sky.

He picked strawberries during the picking season and earned enough money to purchase a large telescope to chart the galaxy night after night. During the summer months, Kirk began clearing some trails to the back of the property. He didn't know how God would use those trails in the years to come.

To add to our family fun, we installed a 20-foot by 40-foot in-ground pool in exchange for the sale of a parcel of our land to a couple whose husband worked for a pool company. As it turned out, the couple got a divorce and didn't want the land, so we had to pay for the pool and got the land back.

Our move to the country was so rewarding to our family. Life was good. We were living the American dream. But one very important thing was missing: Jesus Christ was not part of our lives. We knew very little of God's Word or the Lordship of Christ.

I had received a white Bible when I was confirmed in eighth grade and carried it at my wedding, but I didn't read it. We began attending a church in Berrien Springs quite regularly, but a personal relationship with Christ was foreign to us. Many Sundays after church, Jim and I would remark that we just didn't get anything out of the sermon. We wondered if other people related to what the pastor had preached. Were we and everyone else just pretending? Something was missing, but we just continued to do what everyone else seemed to be doing. We went to church and did what the church said to do – and thought we were Christians.

I didn't know that soon I would receive a wake-up call, and my American dream would be jolted back to reality.

THREE

The Woven Threads of Our Marriage Torn
"I will give you a new heart and put a new spirit in you." – Ezekiel 36:26a

FIVE YEARS INTO THIS VENTURE of living in the country, I was again working hard to achieve and succeed. I knocked the horse hair plaster off the walls of the old farmhouse, carried it out in buckets, and dumped it in the driveway. (Now I know why my back is so bad today.) Then Jim brought the sheets of drywall home from the lumber company and we would complete another room of the 150-year-old house. The process was slow. It was 1975 and many rooms were still not finished.

No one told us to score drywall with a utility knife, so we cut all the wall material with a saber saw. That process had one huge drawback: It produced a large cloud of white dust. So when we remodeled the old kitchen into our family room during the winter months, there was an occasional blizzard going on outside and a huge white dust storm going on inside. We couldn't open the windows or the door because of the blizzard, and we couldn't see each other inside the room to get anything done because of the dust. Besides that, the dust settled on everything inside the house (even on the second story) and it was a mess. It wasn't until the *last* room we worked on in the house that we learned to score the drywall!

At this time in our remodeling project, I got a part-time job at a lumber yard/home center in St. Joseph. It was worth the discount I was able to get on our building materials, but it was not worth what was happening to our marriage. Jim was working at Whirlpool in St. Joseph (sometimes late hours). Then one night my husband said those horrible words I never dreamed I would hear: "I want a divorce."

There were other things going on in his life, and I was totally ignorant of what was happening.

No, no, no this can't be! The word divorce came from the man I'd loved from the first moment I met him. I felt so secure in our marriage. This couldn't be true. Jim was the greatest and most gentle man I had ever met, and I *knew* our marriage would go on forever. How could this be?

My first words to Jim's request for a divorce were: "It can't be. I even make sure you have fresh-baked chocolate chip cookies every week."

Some weeks later, when a marriage counselor asked me why I fell in love with Jim, my answer was, "Because he was such a gentle man." He was everything I wanted in a husband. He wasn't perfect – but neither was I. We seemed to be the most loving couple around. We rarely fought or had harsh words, and I just knew divorce was never going to happen to us! I was so devastated and dazed with unbelief and ignorant of worldly influences in our lives. I would not have been more surprised if a freight train had raced through our living room. It was difficult for me to face the thought of failure because I was so driven to achieve and succeed.

I had so many questions.

What would I do? I couldn't live alone, and I couldn't even *think* about starting all over again. What about Tanya and Kirk? They were just young teens, and this would destroy their expectations of a secure and loving family? What about the house and the farm? At this point, though, I was most concerned about Jim. What was he getting himself into, and how would this mess up his life? He was such a good man. This unbelievable breakup would be such devastation to all of our lives.

There seemed to be no answers to my questions.

In total desperation, I physically ran away from what was facing me. It was autumn, and I ran through fields of rotting tomatoes and prickly weeds that left Velcro-type seeds on the orange double-knit slacks I was wearing. I attempted to find a path in the woods, fighting through prickly berry bushes. I sobbed with all my heart as I ran through a lowland area where we had just had tobogganed down the hill the winter before – as a family. Good times. But now the love of family and the good life I thought we had was fading so rapidly. My adrenaline kept me running and looking for an answer. Six hours later I was ready to finally give up.

I found myself flat on my face on the sun-warmed ground, in a beautiful apple orchard about five miles from our family's home. It was Labor Day 1975, and in tears I gave up. I surrendered and confessed my sin of running my own life, of my pride, of trying to control everything, and demanding that everything be perfect. It was my surrender to a God I really did not know or understand, but this God was working on breaking my spirit. I humbly pleaded with God to take my life from there on and do whatever He had for me. I was indeed searching for the "hidden treasure" in the field in the parable found in Matthew chapter thirteen. The Holy Spirit touched me as my heart was changed forever. He calmed my spirit and gave me hope.

Some months later I was led to a Bible verse that perfectly described this encounter with God: *"My ears had heard of you but now my eyes have seen you. Therefore I despise myself and repent in dust and ashes."* – Job 42:5-6

My heart was seeking a pardon from the Almighty God; a God I didn't really know but felt His love and would soon be so drawn to. I wanted to be His and let go of everything. There was nothing I could do to save my marriage.

God would have to do a miracle in both of us.

FOUR

The Hand of Jesus Christ Touches a Wounded Woman

"Therefore if any man be in Christ, he is a new creature; old things are passed away; all things are become new." – 2 Corinthians 5:17 KJV

I HAVE LONG BELIEVED that right there in that apple orchard, flat on my face, I asked Jesus to be my Lord – months before realizing Him as my Savior. The reference "Lord" appears over 6,000 times in the Bible and "Savior" only 55 times. Most generally Lord appears before Savior, as in "My Lord and Savior". On that Labor Day, I stopped laboring for perfection and laid down my life for my Lord.

I was desperate, and pleaded for Him to forgive me of who I had been. The Holy Spirit had indeed changed my heart, and the control I had prided myself with was now in the hands of a loving God.

I came out of the wooded area and walked down Deans Hill Road, ending up in the emergency room of what was then Berrien General Hospital. I asked for something to help calm me down and help me sleep. I needed help, and knew there were very understanding doctors at the hospital. Some years earlier Kirk had emergency surgery there, and we loved the compassion of the doctors.

A wonderful Christian doctor saw me. I remember he was so gentle and understanding. He encouraged me in the Lord, prayed with me, and told me to continue to show unconditional love to Jim – no matter what was happening day to day. "Dr. A" prayed with me to receive a confidence in God that would fill me with joy and peace.

"Peace I leave with you; my peace I give you. I do not give to you as the world gives. Do not let not your hearts be troubled and do not be afraid." – John

14:27

The love and compassion of the doctors reflected the love and compassion of God. Coming from the emergency room, in my lowest hour, God lovingly showed me that I was as the Apostle Paul states a "chief of sinners" – and Judy had failed. I had failed! I had been running my own life and maybe my husband's too. Everything had to be perfect and, above all, I was proud of who I was and what I could accomplish. My goal was to make it in life.

My children would be the best, the top of the line. In fact when Kirk started high school, he mentioned that we always made him feel like he was so great, and now he realized there were smarter kids and better athletes. He said "Mom, we are not really the greatest!"

I had always thought that I wasn't that bad of a person. I wasn't much of a sinner because I had never done anything *really* bad. I knew about God and believed the Holy Spirit was my conscience, but just couldn't understand the Jesus part: the cross, the blood, and sin.

I was a good person and had always hoped I'd be in heaven when I died. In fact just three years prior to the difficulty in our marriage, I had a discussion with my mother about whether she thought we would go to heaven. I mentioned that we really never had much to do with God except a meal prayer, the bedtime prayer, and church attendance some Sundays. As a child, I do remember my parents saying, "We better go to church this Sunday because we haven't gone in a while." It was not a heart issue. It was a works issue.

I would look for God when we went to church because it was God's house. We had to behave because He had to be there somewhere! To me, that was the only place I could find God, but I found Him in an apple orchard.

Actually God found me.

He found me at my lowest point, on my knees, with my face to the ground, trying to run away from failure – and finally giving up to a God I really didn't know. There I was among the apple trees, heavy-laden with ripe fruit ready to be harvested; an abundant fruit, a result of a dedicated farmer and the Creator of all things.

I, Judy Rose Scofield, was being reborn as a child of God. Jesus touched me and made me whole. I realized I needed to let go of the "I" and let God be the center of my life. I was certainly ready to let go. My life seemed very hopeless. But it was there that God took me in His arms and showed me my sin and my need of a relationship with my Maker. He clearly said, "Let go, Judy, and let Me have control of your life. Give it up."

"For all have sinned and fall short of the glory of God, and are justified freely by his grace through the redemption that came by Christ Jesus." – Romans 3:23-24

I actually had no idea what really happened in the orchard. I just knew I had to let go and turn to God. Out of desperation I placed the future of my life, my marriage, my children, and my Jim in Jesus Christ's hands. I didn't say that perfect sinner's prayer. (I don't believe there *is* one!) Nor did I have anyone there to lead me. I just said, "I have tried to control my own life. God, I have failed and I give up". There would be no more performance-driven life. God gave me the courage to accept His acceptance of me.

I would be at peace within and with God, with Christ in my heart.

☙ ☙ ☙ ☙ ☙ ☙ ☙

God's Word: Mending the Fabric of My Life

"So is my word that goes out from my mouth: It will not return to me empty." – Isaiah 55:11b

In the beginning of my walk with the Lord, I knew very little Scripture. I had memorized some during the seventh and eighth grades of Lutheran School, but I had never learned application. In just one month, I literally wore out a small booklet of uplifting Bible verses by Norman Vincent Peale. It was given to me by an older gentleman, Oscar, who was the accountant where I worked, truly an angel from God. He was indeed a golden thread woven into the tapestry of my conversion. He said his church, First Assembly of God would be praying for me – and they did.

The little booklet was all that I had to hang onto. It helped me memorize Scripture and understand God loved me. I felt very much alone. God's Word continued to confirm His love and promises to me and that He had made me a new creation, a new heart, and a new nature. As St. Augustine once said, *"You have formed us for thyself, and our hearts are restless until they find rest in thee."* I had been very restless all of my life.

Oscar was such a warm hearted Christian and he became very important in my life. I always called him my "Papa in the Lord" because of his wisdom. As I shared the difficulties of my marriage with him, he told me I needed to know Jesus. He was right. I had believed in God and kind of understood the Holy Spirit, but I did not know Jesus as my Savior. God's Word would change all that.

With my little book of Scriptures in one hand, the steering wheel in the other, and tears streaming down my face, I memorized God's promises as I drove the twenty miles back and forth to work each day. I did this for the next three months. The angels were with me or I'd have never found my way safely home. These are a few of the promises of God's Word that I memorized from that booklet to sustain me on my journey (all the verses are KJV):

"...but this one thing I do, forgetting those things which are behind, and reaching forth unto those things which are before. I press toward the mark for the prize of the high calling of God in Christ Jesus." – Philippians 3:13b-14

"Be careful for nothing; but in everything by prayer and supplication with thanksgiving let your requests be made known unto God. And the peace of God, which passes all understanding, shall keep your hearts and minds through Christ Jesus." – Philippians 4:6-7

"Finally, brethren, whatsoever things are true, whatsoever things are honest, whatsoever things are just, whatsoever things are pure, whatsoever things are lovely, whatsoever things are of good report; if there be an virtue, and if there be any praise, think on these things." – Philippians 4:8

"Not that I speak in respect of want: for I have learned, in whatsoever state I am, therewith to be content." – Philippians 4:11

"I can do all things through Christ which strengthens me." – Philippians 4:13 *"(I pray) that he would grant you, according to the riches of his glory, to be strengthened with might by his Spirit in the inner man; That Christ may dwell in your hearts by faith; that ye, being rooted and grounded in love, may be able to comprehend with all saints what is the breadth, and length, and depth, and height; And to know the love of Christ, which passes knowledge, that ye might be filled with all the fullness of God."* – Ephesians 3:16-19

Memorizing God's Word was like placing my feet on solid ground. It held me firm even when depression began to set in. I desperately needed the affirmation of God's Word to keep my head from drowning in despair. I believe when people suffer emotionally so dramatically, they expend so much energy to keep going that eventually they lose all energy – and easily drop into a pit of depression.

As God was healing me, the brokenness in my marriage continued. Jim was in and out of our lives at this point and really struggled with where his devotion belonged. As I drove back and forth to my job, I would sing "Jesus Loves Me" with the tears in my eyes flowing down my cheeks. It was the only song I knew. I sang at the top of my lungs, constantly reaffirming that *He did* love me and would take care of me and my family.

I tried to keep our family together, to continually love my husband, and encourage my children. "No matter what, we will show Daddy that no one can love him as much as we do – and Jesus loves him too."

❧ ❧ ❧ ❧ ❧ ❧ ❧

Mending the Family

"And the vessel that he made of clay was marred in the hand of the potter: so he made it again another vessel, as seemed good to the potter to make." – Jeremiah 18:4 KJV

I was a woman desperate to save my marriage. I would do anything to show my love to keep Jim. I prayed daily, and sometimes I felt it was all day long. Life at this time had multiple ups and downs, and many times I just wanted to give up.

After three agonizing months of not knowing our future direction, God began doing a wonderful work in Jim's heart. Jim was finally willing to go to counseling with me, and I felt confident that he wanted to go the extra mile and make our relationship work. It was our second attempt to start over, and Jim would be calling the shots.

Jim wanted me to make some changes in my life; maybe dress younger and spend more time with him. He wanted us to take a vacation – just the two of us. It would be so good to spend time together without the children. I hesitated because we had never done anything like that before. But soon we took our pickup camper and headed north, leaving our two young teens with Jim's parents. It was a wise decision because we needed uninterrupted, quality time together.

In the midst of trying to hold my marriage together, I had alienated my parents – or so they thought. My father wanted to step in and talk to Jim. I had asked both of them not to get involved, and they misunderstood my intentions. My parents felt that I wanted them to stay away and not see their grandchildren anymore. Oh how this hurt! I needed their love and support, and they were angry and very harsh with me.

Our relationship was still fragile when Jim came back home, and we began to rebuild our marriage. My parents remained feeling alienated, and Dad said that Mom cried every night. This misunderstanding took *months* to reconcile, but eventually peace and love prevailed.

"Blessed is the man who perseveres under trial, because when he has stood the test, he will receive the crown of life that God has promised to those who love him." – James 1:12

FIVE

A New Direction in Our Lives

"Now to Him who is able to do immeasurably more than all we ask or imagine, according to His power that is at work within us." – Ephesians 3:20

DURING OUR TURBULENT THREE MONTHS, Tanya (a freshman in high school) met a very godly young man (a senior) at band camp. She became involved, through his direction, in a Bible quizzing youth group and through this ministry became a Christian. Tanya encouraged us to change churches and attend her home church just down a country road from where we lived: Berrien Center Bible Church.

The first Sunday that we attended as a family was a special service. They featured a young couple, who were in the recording business. They shared their music and testimony of God's work in their lives through a recent dark time.

The young couple had conceived twins and carried them to full term, but only one of the babies survived. As the mother shared how God had gently walked her through this tragedy, I realized He was doing the same with us. I realized God wanted us to have that same relationship with Him. I cried throughout the entire service, and I remember Tanya saying, "its okay, Mom. This is a good place. It's alright to cry here." God was in this mother's life, He was in this church, and He so desperately wanted to be in our lives.

Tanya's friend was a shining thread in our Tapestry, and he still shines in our lives and ministry today. God used this young man and a beautiful testimony to open our eyes to God's faithfulness during our times of need.

For the next couple of years, we devoured everything we could get our hands on to read and listen to, trying to understand what God wanted of our lives. As we drove home from church each Sunday, we would remark how our pastor's sermon was just for us. God was speaking to us! Never before had we understood Scripture and how God used His Word to direct lives. We began to understand that God had a purpose and a plan for our lives. We were seeking answers to what that plan might be.

During this exciting time in our lives, though, I was increasingly fighting bouts of depression. The highs and lows of the past six months had taken a toll on my stability. One day as Jim and I were walking through a mall, we stopped by a music store and happened to pick out an 8-track tape in the gospel music section by Bill and Gloria Gaither. (For those younger readers, you may need to Google "8-track tape" if you're not sure what that is!)

At the time, we had no idea who the Gaithers were or what Christian music was like, but their music brought stability to my heart. It was a "God thing", a vertical thread He wove to keep our lives focused on Him. I can still hear André Crouch's words as the Gaithers sang, "Through It All", and how it ministered to me. The words of the third verse are still so significant in my life today:

I thank God for the mountains, And I thank Him for the valleys / I thank Him for the storms He's brought me through / For if I never had a problem, I wouldn't know that He could solve them / I'd never know what faith in God could do. / Through it all, through it all, I've learned to trust in Jesus, I've learned to trust in God / Through it all, through it all, I've learned to depend upon His Word.

I nearly wore that 8-track tape out. The music filled the hurt in my heart with the love of Jesus. From sunrise to sundown, the wonderful uplifting songs gave me so much hope. Bill and Gloria's song "He Touched Me" helped me erase the guilt I had in the failures of my life: *"He touched me and made me whole"*. That is what I experienced as I ran away from my problems and surrendered in the orchard on that Labor Day. I had placed my life in His hands and I was His. He had made me whole – a new person in Christ.

The songs reaffirmed what God continued to teach me through his Word. God loved me and He loved Jim, and we would make it together. God's Word gave me hope. Jim was a very understanding husband to my struggles. Every night we spent hours, sometimes almost all night, reading God's Word and talking about what He might have planned for our lives. It was all so new to us and so exciting. We now had a new life with new meaning, and we prayed for God's new direction for us.

"Therefore if any man be in Christ, he is a new creature; old things are passed away; behold, all things are become new." – 2 Corinthians 5:17 KJV

ℜ ℜ ℜ ℜ ℜ ℜ ℜ

A Historic Thread of Letting Go and Trusting

"Commit your way to the Lord, trust also in Him, and He shall bring it to pass."
Psalm 37:5 NKJV

In the summer of 1976, Tanya went on a six-week mission trip with Teen Missions International to Cape Haitian, Haiti. It was indeed a growing time for all of us. Before Christ came into our lives, we would not have imagined letting our 16-year-old daughter go for six weeks with an organization we only knew about through an ad in a Christian magazine. But she belonged to God, and we were only here to raise her – a totally new concept of parental release.

One summer day in July, we drove Tanya to Detroit to board a bus with many other teens headed for the Teen Missions Boot Camp in Florida. It was so much about her faith and her willingness to serve. God introduced another thread into our Tapestry, and Tanya's faith taught us to let go and trust; something that would be important as the Tapestry was beginning to take shape. It was indeed a thread of trust and dying to self.

At that time there were no cell phones or e-mail, and her letters arrived two weeks after she wrote them. It was a long six weeks. I would go out in the front yard, look up into the heavens and pray, knowing that the same God who was watching over me was watching over her. I could trust Him.

Tanya's experience was life-changing. She and the other teens lived in tents, showered under a water spout with a plastic covering around it, and experienced practically no privacy for restroom needs. They were roughing it big time during this extremely physical challenge.

Tanya's group of twenty teens built a school for an orphanage in Cape Haitian. They laid cement blocks, tied off irons, and mixed cement by hand. Some days they ran out of cement, blocks, or mortar and prayed for their supplies. During their last week, they laid a roof on the first story and prepared it for a second story to be put on by another team. These twenty teens carried the cement up the ladders in coffee cans.

Tanya's experience not only changed her life, but it impacted Jim and me as well. The entire Haiti experience began a thirst in us for a ministry to challenge youth. We began to see the value of stretching young people to grow their faith in Christ.

The first night back in the states, Tanya laid in bed sobbing. I was surprised and when I asked her why, she said, "The people in Haiti had nothing but were always singing and happy. Here in America we have everything, but people don't care about each other and no one is happy." Her eyes had been opened to the real meaning of life. We now had a thread of hope that we might someday serve Him by being involved in something like Teen Missions.

I will quote this statement from a Dutch theologian named Edward Schillebeeckx often in my life because it is what *Tapestry* is about: *"Christianity is not a message which has to be believed, but an experience of faith which becomes a message."* Jim and I were on the brink of an experience that would be a powerful message to us – and many others as well.

"And He died for all, that those who live should no longer live for themselves but for him who died for them and was raised again." – 2 Corinthians 5:15

"Then said Jesus unto his disciples, If any man will come after me, let him deny himself, and take up his cross, and follow me. For whosoever will save his life shall lose it: and whosoever will lose his life for my sake shall find it. For what is a man profited, if he shall gain the whole world, and lose his own soul? Or what shall a man give in exchange for his soul? – Matthew 16:24-26 KJV

For the next two years after Tanya's mission experience, we searched the Scriptures and prayed: "God, what do you want of our lives?" Might He want us to go to the mission field? But where and what could we do? Jim was not a pastor or a doctor. Our mindset was that all missionaries were either doctors or pastors! We had no training, and we certainly were not Bible intellects.

Then one Sunday, a missionary from Trans World Radio spoke at our church. He was a tower man on the island of Borneo. He had previously worked in the states as a lineman for the electric company, and God was using him with his abilities on the mission field. This was indeed an eye-opener. Could there be a place for us in missions? What might that be, Lord? Scripture kept speaking to us, and God knew the desire of our hearts. The timing would be His, and we would continue to listen to His leading.

"For we are God's workmanship, created in Christ Jesus to do good works ..." – Ephesians 2:10a

These new thoughts kept going through our minds. Everything we read or listened to seemed to say the same thing: yield to God. But what did yield really mean?

SIX

God's 100-Year Thread: 1876 and 1976

"Set your affection on things above, not on things on the earth." – Colossians 3:2
KJV

THINKING BACK through the beginning of our spiritual journey, Jim and I sat down together in 1976 and released our lives and Five Pines Farm to the Lord. We recalled expressing to God our desire that He would use the land and our lives to further the Gospel to those around us. Unknown to us at the time, *it was exactly 100 years ago* in 1876 when Great Grandpa Albert Murphy and his wife Sarah Jane made their decision to release their lives, their possessions, and dedicate the rest of their days to proclaim the Gospel however God would lead them.

In Great Grandpa Albert's words from his journal: *"The next day after I had pledged with my wife, and had gone through the excruciating ordeal of meeting God's just claim on my life, was the darkest day of my life … Among the things that became new was a great desire that all the world might know what the Lord had done for me and the beautiful harmony of Scripture. And it was a joy to see that Paul and John Wesley could not have taught what they did, had they not met the Lord on His wise and loving conditions that made them willing to be as 'sheep for the slaughter'."*

One hundred years later, God spoke to Jim and me from Matthew chapter 14. The disciples were in a little fishing vessel being tossed about by a raging storm. Fear overwhelmed their hearts until Jesus appeared walking on the water and said, *"Take courage! It is I. Don't be afraid."*

Then Peter replied, *"Lord if it's you, tell me to come to you on the water."* Peter *immediately* stepped out of the boat and walked on the water. As Peter began to sink and cry out to Jesus, He reached out His hand and said, *"You of little faith, why do you doubt?"* (from Matthew 14:27-31).

Was God asking us to step out of the "boat"? Was He saying to let go and come to Him? If God was asking us to get out of the boat, He was also asking us not to doubt where He wanted us to go and what and how He wanted us to do it.

As we read an earlier Matthew passage, we began to understand: *"Do not store up for yourselves treasures on the earth, where moth and rust destroy, and where thieves break in and steal. But store up for yourselves treasures in heaven, where moth and rust do not destroy, and where thieves do not break in and steal. For where your treasure is, there your heart will be also"* (Matthew 6:19-21).

It had now become not just a faith issue, but a heart issue. To let go and step out of the boat meant a total surrender of our hearts. It was seeing the ministry of Jesus and how we related to it through the eyes of our hearts. O ye of little faith!

"No one can serve two masters. Either he will hate the one and love the other, or he will be devoted to the one and despise the other. You cannot serve both God and Money. Therefore I tell you, do not worry about your life, what you will eat or drink; or about your body, what you will wear. Is not life more important than food, and the body more important than clothes?" – Matthew 6:24-25.

Our prayer became, "God make our lives meaningful and use us." Not really knowing what that meant, we sought God's will for our lives (but with many doubts). Was our faith strong enough to accomplish what God wanted us to do? This statement by E.M. Bounds, which I read later, expressed our heart's desire: "We are to be a golden pipe through which oil flows."

Great Grandpa Albert also questioned his faith and abilities. In his words: *"My Christian experience was so satisfactory that when I heard other Christians professing a second work of Grace I believed they were reclaimed from a backslidden condition, but I could see that they were real Christians and manifested a better spirit than their oppressors. It was not a great while that I noticed that some of Charles Wesley's hymns floated above where I could reach, and my inner experience did perfectly not harmonize with the teachings of Jesus and Paul. But I was delighted and encouraged when I found that Jesus said, 'Blessed are they which do hunger and thirst after righteousness for they shall be filled' and 'If ye abide in me and my words abide in you ye shall ask what ye will and it shall be done unto you.'"*

ᘐ ᘐ ᘐ ᘐ ᘐ ᘐ ᘐ

Weaving Biblical Principles

"All Scripture is God-breathed and is useful for teaching, rebuking, correcting and training in righteousness." – 2 Timothy 3:16

As we continued to search for God's direction, our church encouraged some of its members to attend a one-week seminar in Grand Rapids. The seminar was entitled Basic Youth Conflicts, and the speaker was Bill Gothard. We thought it was Bill Gaither, so we thought we would sign up and go since we liked his music. God was again weaving a powerful vertical thread into our Tapestry: the principles of the Word of God.

Of course, it turned out not to be Bill Gaither and his music, but a deeply convicting seminar on the principles of God's Word and how they apply to our lives. Jim rededicated his life to the Lord there and was more willing than ever to do what God wanted him to do. In fact, it was so convicting that we took a van of young people up to Grand Rapids for the seminar for seven years in a row! That seminar taught applicable lessons to us and to the young people that God eventually brought into our lives.

I remember so vividly the story of the father, who week after week promised his son he'd take him fishing, but business conflicts arose and he always let his son down. The seminar charted year after year the broken promises, as the root of rebellion became very evident in the son's life. Eventually the son was in deep trouble with the law, and his root of rebellion led him there.

This was our first impression that God's Word applies to *everything* in life. We were being grounded in God's Word and His principles. Basic Youth Conflicts opened our eyes to finally understand that God's Word contains all you need to know about life and how to live. The seminar was another vertical thread God used to begin the Tapestry. The main thread woven was very simple: His Word is Truth, we are all sinners in need of a Savior, and He has a plan for each of our lives.

Time and time again Jesus is referred to in God's Word as Lord and Savior – as Lord of our lives. He is someone who demands ownership and an unquestionable right to command our lives. Not only did He die for our sins, but He was asking Jim and me to surrender to Him as Lord.

To be happy in life, we understood that pride in a performance-driven life was not of God. God meant for each of us to "abide in Him" in everything we do. Once again, He was asking us to let go and put our lives in Him and trust Him *fully*. God and God alone wanted to make the beautiful tapestry of our lives and a ministry called Five Pines. LET GO of everything, the farm, the land and our lives and LET ME do what I have planned for your lives.

"Do you not know that your body is a temple of the Holy Spirit ... You are not your own; you were bought at a price." – 1 Corinthians 6:19-20a

God's chosen people were slaves to the Egyptians for hundreds of years and were finally released to worship and serve the one true God. We were once slaves to sin, but now we have been purchased by a new Master who bought us with a most costly price – His Son. We were now released from the bondage of sin to worship and serve as a bond slave to the Lordship of Jesus Christ. Jim and I slowly began to realize what it meant to become a Christian.

"For none of us lives to himself alone and none of us dies to himself alone. If we live, we live to the Lord; and if we die, we die to the Lord. So, whether we live or die, we belong to the Lord." – Romans 14:7-9

We began to add things up:
• We had inherited the farm from Jim's family.

- God was calling us to be faithful with what He had given us.
- Neither of us had a college degree or any special talent, but God had given Jim the uncanny wisdom and knowledge you can only receive working as a farmer. (Knowledge and common sense that is still so very valuable today.) If God called us, He would provide. He would equip.

SEVEN

A Major Thread: Releasing the Farm

"Since, then, you have been raised with Christ, set your hearts on things above, where Christ is seated at the right hand of God. Set your minds on things above, not on earthly things."– Colossians 3:1-2

IN MATTHEW 25, Jesus taught his disciples with a word picture of the man who entrusted his possessions to his servants. When the owner of the property returned, he expected to be pleased with what they had done in managing his estate.

But what did that mean to Jim and Judy? What did God want of this land? How could we share the principles in God's precious Word with the land we had? How could God use a run-down farm, a run-down barn, and two very simple people without any dreams of possibilities? God had given us a passion: young people. Now we began to seek His purpose and plan.

"But the people that do know their God shall be strong, and do exploits." – *Daniel 11:32b KJV*

Jim felt God had given him a very strong desire to share this old farm with other people – but how? He wanted to somehow encourage churches and youth groups to use our thirty-plus acres of land. It had become *total wilderness* though. Where at one time peach orchards once thrived, now trees, berry bushes, and shrubs made it impossible to find a path!

In 1977, Jim thought maybe it would be fun to run hayrides and then afterwards have a bonfire. He borrowed hay wagons and tractors from nearby farmers and eventually raised some money to purchase three wagons at an auction. There was a place on our farm, not too far from the old barn, where years ago the county road commission dug out gravel from a small hill to use on the dirt roads. It formed a perfect place for a fire circle.

One weekend, a couple who were youth leaders at Berrien Center Bible Church came over to help dig out a fire pit. Jim got on his Snapper mower to mow a trail north from the old barn and across the field to the place of the old gravel pit. The field was thick with boysenberry bushes and sumac trees.

The three of us stood on the hill at the far end of the field and watched Jim on that Snapper mower knock down everything in its way and "bulldoze" a trail through the field. The bushes in the field were so dense that we couldn't even see Jim on the mower! I remember it sounded and looked like a tank clearing the path as the sumac trees fell left and right, and the boysenberry bushes were vanquished.

Our first fire in the new pit was for the Berrien Center Bible Church youth group. It was a great night, and visions of what God might do excited us. Our new fire pit was just west of a magnificently beautiful old maple tree, and thus came the name of Maple Glen Fire Circle. This was the first landmark on what was to be Five Pines Ministries.

Jim was excited. This was part of his vision of God's use of the land. It was the start of our hayride program, but would people come besides our home church youth group? Only time would tell.

EIGHT

Seven Godly Men

"I became a servant of this gospel by the gift of God's grace given me through the working of his power. Although I am less than the least of all God's people ..." –
Ephesians 3:7-8a

THE HAYRIDE PROGRAM was the beginning of many miracles and a confirmation God was going to do some extraordinary things in our lives and on the farmland. We were beginning to watch the threads of the tapestry weave together.

If Jim was going to raise money for things like the hay wagons, we needed advice and direction. It was time to establish a board of directors, work on incorporation papers, and apply for a 501(c)(3) tax designation.

The board of directors would come first. Jim began to pray for God's direction to men who would be willing to serve on a board of a non-profit Christian youth organization. In 1978, after much prayer, Jim felt led to seek out seven Godly men (patterned after Acts 6). Jim and I were rather new in the Lord and knew few believers. We had very little idea where to begin – but God did.

God helped Jim to step out in faith and led him first to one prospective board member, and that person suggested another person – and so it went. He knocked on doors of some people he had never met before. Imagine trying to "sell" an idea to someone you didn't know, and you really weren't sure what it was going to be! Jim was not a pastor, a teacher, or a Bible school graduate. But he did share this with prospective board members: "I have thirty-three acres of land and feel God leading me into this rather unknown endeavor."

I had just begun working part-time at Southwestern Medical Clinic and was impressed with Don Gast, the executive director. Don was a very special man with a heart of gold. He always believed in people and was sensitive to their needs. He loved the Lord and sat on many organizational boards in the Southwestern Michigan area. I suggested to Jim that he should go talk to Don, whom he did not know. Don was excited about the possibility of a youth ministry and agreed to be involved.

Over the years, Don was the most supportive person in the ministry. He indeed was the giant of anyone God brought into our lives over the past thirty-five years. He wore his love for Jim and me, for the ministry, and for God on the outside of his heart. The value of his involvement is beyond imagination. He indeed was one of the most important threads in our Tapestry.

In focusing on other prospective board members, Don suggested that Jim talk to a local gentleman who had been involved in youth ministries across the country, and he said yes. Don also knew we would need a lawyer for the incorporation papers and suggested an attorney. He was willing to sit on the board and help us get everything started. There was also a dynamic Christian man who was a local realtor in Berrien Springs who Jim approached and he was eager to join the board. Lastly the names of two former pastors were also introduced to Jim and both of them were eager to join Jim's board. Jim then became the seventh board member.

God had done a marvelous work in bringing the board together. The basic pattern of the Tapestry was beginning to take shape. God wove seven Godly men together as vertical threads to begin the story of a new ministry.

Over the years, all of these original board members have been ever so faithful. Bill Wurzel had served on the board for almost thirty years. Don Gast was a faithful board member for over thirty-five years, and many of the other original board members still support the ministry. God had demonstrated His faithfulness, answered our prayers, and blessed us beyond any human understanding. God's leading in supplying the seven men for our original board reaffirmed our faith and led us to commit ourselves more deeply. As the years moved on, we would see God weave people in and out of this ministry for such a time as was needed and then move them on.

Hebrews 11:8 says that Abraham *"obeyed and went, even though he did not know where he was going."* That described Jim in 1978, but his faith was the key to many miracles. It was nothing short of a miracle that these six men were willing to sit on a board of a new ministry they basically knew nothing about and be led by a man they hardly knew!

We were still at the stage of asking God what He would do with this land and two willing people who wanted to serve Him. We only knew that *God* knew what He was going to accomplish, and Jim trusted Him entirely. *If the ministry developed and became successful, it would be about God. If it didn't, it would still be about God.* He had revealed to us who He is, and God's Word repeatedly and explicitly stated that we were created to serve Him.

Many Bible stories told of God using the least, the last, and the lost. We seemed to fit in those categories. It seemed plain and simple: God was saying let go and let Me! In a sense it sounded both very simple and very difficult. In actuality, it was simpler than one would believe. What did we have to lose?

"Verily I say unto you, whatsoever ye shall bind on earth shall be bound in heaven; and whatsoever ye shall loose on earth shall be loosed in heaven." – Matthew 18:18 KJV

I like a quote from John Piper on his church's mission statement: *"Bethlehem (Baptist Church) exists to spread a passion for the supremacy of God in all things for the joy of all peoples through Jesus Christ."* We felt that God wanted that same approach in this ministry.

Five Pines was just in the infancy of its ministry, and this group of men spent many hours discussing what direction God was leading. Each offered prayers to God on how He wanted to use this land, minister to families, and have a heavy focus on youth. Because of Tanya's challenging experience in Haiti with Teen Missions, we had formulated the desire to challenge young people both physically and especially spiritually. The board also suggested Five Pines be a ministry for local youth and activities like the hayrides and maybe wilderness trips for groups. They discussed a daycare center, but it never materialized.

Finally, in 1979, Five Pines Christian Family Center was established as a non-profit organization with incorporation papers. The board of directors voted on the Five Pines title because the farm had always been known as Five Pines Farm. (Jim's great, great, great Grandfather Orin D. Snow planted five white pines in the front yard of the original home.)

After the formation of a board of directors and receiving our incorporation papers, God began to bring people and ideas into our lives. An additional "giant in the faith" came onto the board: Dr. Bob. Jim had a desire to someday have a retreat center, and he envisioned it near the back of the property. In that location, it would have a beautiful wooded setting and wonderful view of the lower land that was full of springs (and had the possibility of being a lake). Dr. Bob and Jim faithfully met every Saturday morning for two years, praying and believing that God would somehow provide the finances.

All this time I felt that God wanted us to work with and minister to people before He would entrust us with buildings. Our prayers became a waiting game now – waiting on God's perfect timing.

ℨ ℨ ℨ ℨ ℨ ℨ

Director Jim Scofield – a Simple Man

"Delight yourself in the Lord and he will give you the desires of your heart." – Psalm 37:4 NASB

I was raised in the city and had a very limited knowledge of the life of anyone who lived, worked, and survived on the land as a farmer. After being married to Jim for fifty-nine years, I now realize how the wisdom of a farming background equipped him not only for life, but to direct a camp ministry as well.

• *A deep understanding of the weather.* The wind direction affected our lives in different ways, whether it was from the north, south, east, or west – or any combination. What did the moon phases mean? What did a clear night mean for the next day? How much of a danger is lightning? How do dry times or too much rain affect programming or lawn care or building projects? Jim made some very important decisions based on this knowledge from God.

• *A basic understanding of almost everything else.* Jim could identify the different trees and whether they were hardwoods or softwoods. He had some valuable knowledge in the areas of machinery, carpentry, and electrical. He may not always have had the ability to fix everything, but he understood what was wrong and what had to be done to get it fixed. God supplied many people who generously stepped in to help Jim keep everything working at Five Pines.

There was no diploma from some fine university in Jim's office. Nothing on the wall told you of his wisdom, his common sense, and the basic life skills that God used to equip him to direct this small ministry in its early years. Nothing on the wall said, "This man trusted God", but he did. Jim believed that our lives had a purpose, and we would find that purpose as we obeyed and were willing to serve Him.

"And now, O Israel, what does the Lord your God ask of you but to fear the Lord your God, to walk in all His ways, to love him, to serve the Lord your God with all your heart and soul." – Deuteronomy 10:12

Jim had lived in the community all his life and was well-respected. His father served as the township clerk and people had highly respected him and his family. Jim exemplified a trustworthy man, and this allowed him to have many connections and the benefit of many experts in the small community of Berrien Springs and the surrounding areas. God provided many of our needs through these connections.

God used a gentle man, equipped him, and gave him wisdom to lead for twenty-eight years. Jim so delighted in the Lord and what the Lord was doing in his life and the land God wanted him to release to Him.

Jim decided early on in the ministry that everything he did would be the very best in the eyes of the community. He kept the grounds beautiful. Lawns were weed-free, watered, and mowed meticulously with the vision of an emerald green carpet. Fields were kept mowed as well, and flowers also helped grace the campgrounds with God's beauty.

This took hours and hours out of Jim's day. Many weekends he spent on the tractor mowing the large fields if our dear friend, Claire, a retired farmer, couldn't make it over. But it was worth it. Our guests would remark how everything looked so nice. It was a work of his heart and a ministry to the Lord.

So with Jim's wisdom and leadership and six godly men by his side, we ventured into our first outreach program.

NINE

Youth Ministry Programs Begin – 1978

"I am come that they might have life, and that they might have it more abundantly."
– John 10:10b KJV

OUR PASSION AND DESIRE to help teens became the driving force God used to help us have a ministry focus. Our burden was based on the knowledge that divorce was prevalent in numerous families, and we knew many teens were hurting – even in church families.

Our son, Kirk, mentioned that he wasn't surprised when divorce became the issue in our family. He said, "At school it is happening to all of my friends, and I figured sooner or later it would happen to ours."

We wanted to help young people find the peace that only God offers and to learn early in their lives what He teaches in His Word.

"Peace I leave with you; my peace I give you. I do not give to you as the world gives. Do not let your hearts be troubled and do not be afraid." – John 14:27

It seemed fitting that before Christ came into our own lives, we were very performance driven. We realized that too many teens were also under pressure to achieve. We wanted our message to be clear that the world had *nothing* to offer, and Christ's peace had *everything* to offer. We chose John 10:10 as our life and ministry verse because a life in Christ is full and exciting, rewarding and satisfying. Nothing can compare.

We were anxious to begin programs for teens in the area. The meetings would have to be in our home, since we didn't have any buildings. So we informed area churches that we wanted to start a non-denominational group of young people who maybe didn't have a youth group in their church. Since our background was from a denominational church, we were hoping to bring young people from all denominations together.

We set a date and time to meet in our home. Ignorantly we expected to have all clean cut "church" kids come! A half hour before the scheduled meeting time, there was a knock at the front door. When I opened the door, there stood two of the most ragamuffin teens I had ever seen – certainly not what I had expected. I remember saying in my mind, *"Not these kinds of kids, Lord."* The two girls had long straight hair, army fatigues on, and a pack of cigarettes rolled up in their sleeves.

As Lori and Kelly (not their real names) came into our living room and sat down, we listened to their stories. It wasn't long before we realized they needed more than our love – they needed the love of Jesus. Their dad was not around because he was a career serviceman, and they basically didn't know him.

These two girls seemed tough on the outside, but were very fragile on the inside. The older girl, Kelly, was a senior and had plans to go into the military to eventually be an auto mechanic. (We later found out that she knew absolutely *nothing* about vehicles and didn't pass auto mechanic technical school!) It was a very interesting first day for us.

Other young people came, and the next day a mother called and said, "I thought this youth group was supposed to be for Christians!" It was a beginning, and God had taught us many things that first night. From that time on, we applied a statement that we learned from a dear friend, Dr. Bob, one of the originators of Southwestern Medical Clinic. He always said, "Our doors will be open to the people whom God created and Jesus Christ died for." That meant everyone.

Since we began meeting every week after the football and basketball games, it was easier to meet in town at a local church that had more room. God provided another vertical strand to our tapestry: a place to meet. Our small group grew and so did our programming.

We took a van load of teens to the week-long youth conflict seminar in Grand Rapids, and Lori signed up to go. Monday through

Thursday was just evening sessions, and we drove back and forth each evening. Friday and Saturday were all day sessions, so we stayed Thursday and Friday nights in a dorm home at a Christian college. The seminar sessions began to dig deep into what our relationships were like – especially between parents and children. Lori struggled with the Biblical principles that were being applied. On Thursday night after the evening sessions, we all sat around discussing the day. Lori said, "What about what my dad said to my sister when she left to go into the service?" She explained that he had left a note on her sister's suitcase which read, "Give them b....... hell!" Lori was angry that her father had left such a horrible note.

I said that he may have been trying to express his concern for Kelly. Maybe he was trying to tell her he loved her and to take care of herself. This was way too much for Lori to accept, and she ran into the kitchen and sobbed. She couldn't comprehend that her father might love her.

Two years later when Lori went away to college, she faithfully wrote to her father and signed every letter, "Love, Lori". Some years later, she drove up to our home with a smile from one ear to the other. She had received a letter from her dad, one of many he had sent her. But this one was signed, "Love, Dad". God had done a tremendous work in her heart.

At one point in her life, Lori had lived with us and had been "one of our kids". We were the parents that she longed to have. She was a very different individual. We never knew what to expect, but God demonstrated His love through us. We shared the Lord with her, our home with her, and learned to love a very unique young lady. She came out and helped us with hayrides and our youth programs for years. Lori was indeed a colorful horizontal thread in this ministry.

Another important colorful thread was about to enter our lives and expand our youth outreach program in an adventurous way.

TEN

Wilderness Weavings

"Call to me and I will answer you and tell you great and unsearchable things you do not know." – Jeremiah 33:3

ABOUT THIS TIME, God brought a young physician named Dr. Richard Roach into the Tapestry picture. He was new on staff at Southwestern Medical Clinic, and he was an avid believer in wilderness camping. Don Gast said, "I believe I know a man you need to meet." Don introduced us, and we recognized that God was providing another very dynamic person to help further Jim's dreams and a clear answer to Jim's prayers.

Dr. Roach became a dear friend, a dynamic board member, and the inspiration to our wilderness trips program. Both he and his wife had worked at a camp in northern Minnesota and were experts at packing food and supplies for trip camps. They were an extremely enthusiastic couple whom we grew to love. They added a tremendous inspiration to this young ministry and very colorful threads to the Tapestry.

Richard was a storyteller, and he excited our hearts with his stories of adventure and ministry. Whatever trip he took, we would just sit and be enthralled by his stories. We thirsted for those experiences of using God's beautiful creation to teach Biblical life lessons. Richard could weave Scriptural meanings into almost any experience, and devotions on his trips were very spontaneous. He took an experience, good or bad, and applied Scriptural teachings to help the group see God's hand in everything.

Dr. Richard Roach was a colorful addition to our lives, one we could not put a value on. He taught us so very much and continually challenged us with new ideas. His love of Scripture added to our own thirst to know God's Word and to always be ready, no matter what the situation, to give an answer to anyone God brought into our lives.

ℬ ℬ ℬ ℬ ℬ ℬ ℬ

Everglade Canoe Trip – Winter of 1980
"Trust in the Lord with all your heart ... and he will make your paths straight." –
Proverbs 3:5-6

Five Pines purchased canoes, and a canoe trailer, in 1980. We planned a Christmas break trip to Florida to canoe the Everglades. Jim had also purchased a bus fully-equipped with kitchen, restroom, and booths with tables that converted into bunks. We were able to make canvas hammocks to hang over the tables, adding to the sleeping space. The plans were coming together.

Our main concern was: "Were the Everglades a safe place to explore?" Kirk was an intern at Sarett Nature Center, so we made an appointment to discuss our plans with the chief naturalist. Our questions revolved around the challenges and dangers we might encounter. He simply commented that it would be pretty easy going and not to worry about snakes or gators. He said we would see lots of birds, and probably the worst thing that could happen was that two kids could get in a fight.

(NOTE: The condition of the growth of gators and pythons has totally changed the Everglades since our trip, and I doubt that such a trip would be recommended today.)

Our church had just hired a new young youth pastor named Art. Since his parents lived in Florida, he was willing to help drive the bus down, stay with his parents for the holiday week, and then help drive the bus back home to Michigan.

For me, this would again be a huge step of faith. I was not a swimmer because I was raised with a fear of water. My mother often mentioned her nightmares of one of her children drowning. Rather than have us take swimming lessons, Mother tried to discourage us from going to the beach or near the water. When Jim and I were dating and my father found out that he owned a canoe, he made it very clear that any canoe was not seaworthy.

Now here we were: Jim, Tanya, Kirk and myself would be on a trip in canoes out into coastal waters! I was again being told by God, "Let go and trust Me!" I had to remember that I belonged to God, and my life was His. This was a big step I couldn't control, and a very important thread called "trust" was added to our Tapestry.

Our adventure would be for thirteen days with thirteen people on the trip. The recently purchased canoe trailer had the five canoes secured onto it, and Jim attached the tongue of the trailer to the back of the bus. It seemed very fragile and kind of held together with duct tape, but we were fearless and trusting in our early adventure.

We left a frigid Michigan with dreams of sun and fun in the southernmost part of Florida – the Everglades. The trip down was uneventful with the exception of my fear of losing the canoes as I watched them bump up and down on the canoe trailer. I was sure we would lose one or two canoes along the way, but we didn't.

At our first stop, just over the state line of Florida, an extremely excited young man named Mark jumped out of the bus and attempted to climb to the top of the first palm tree he had ever seen. As it turned out, Mark's enthusiasm magnified itself as the trip progressed.

We proceeded to drive down the long state of Florida and eventually dropped Art off at his parent's house. From there we drove to Homestead to make a southwest turn into Everglades National Park. We were three hours from Flamingo, our destination and the southernmost visitor center.

Just before we made the turn, the tongue of the canoe trailer broke. We had no way of fixing it, so what would we do? We were basically out in the middle of nowhere. Prayer seemed the only answer, and we needed this to become God's problem – not ours. So our bus was on the side of the road with a broken canoe trailer and thirteen people praying. Remember it was *way* before cell phones. Soon after, a car stopped and the driver told us that there was a trucking company about a half mile down the road, and they may be able to weld it.

We tied the tongue of the trailer up, had some of our teens watch the trailer out the back window, and headed down the road *slowly* to the trucking company. When we arrived, the gentleman there said, "If it stops raining, I might see what I can do." So we sat on the bus and prayed for another hour. We prayed and it continually rained a long Florida afternoon rain. The guy in the trucking company probably thought we were crazy.

Well, God was faithful. The rain stopped after an hour, the man decided he could weld the tongue, and soon we were headed down the highway again. Had the canoe trailer tongue broken two or three miles later, we would have been in the middle of swamp land and nowhere near "civilization" and a welder. To top it off, the trucking company didn't charge us anything. This was indeed one of many teaching moments we would learn as the trip progressed. We praised the Lord because He again was so faithful. We added another strand of faith and answered prayer to our Tapestry.

Our group settled in at the Flamingo campground, site thirteen, which seemed to be our lucky number: thirteen people gone for thirteen days and camping on site number thirteen. Our anxious group of teens soon decided to venture out into Flamingo Bay in three canoes. As they moved out into the bay, Kirk spotted what looked like a large eagle's nest high in a mangrove tree. With much enthusiasm all three canoes were speedily paddled towards the island. In their exuberance they failed to read the "Do not enter" signs on either side of the island!

From almost out of nowhere, a kayak with a park ranger entered the picture in hot pursuit. We had six young people in deep trouble. The fine was $50 a person, and we did not have the $300 to pay the fine. Finally the park ranger agreed to have the six young people do community service work and pick up trash on a mosquito-infested road on the back side of the park. Kirk had interned at two nature centers, and he knew the law about the protection of an eagle's nest. In the excitement of it all, though, he just forgot. We were all learning so much.

The next day we loaded up our backpacks, canoes, food, and water. We were to canoe through the man-made Bear Lake Canoe Channel, twenty-seven miles round trip to Cape Sable, and out to the southernmost coast of Florida. It was a seven-hour trip and would take us through mangrove swamps with lots of beautiful birds and more than its share of mosquitoes. We soon realized that if you had any part of your body that wasn't covered with high-powered bug spray, you were a meal for the mosquitoes. We saw no one along the way and no gators or snakes. (The naturalist was right.) The day was cool and the fresh-water canal very narrow, shallow, and swampy. When we canoed nearer to the coast, we had a small dike to portage into salt water.

After seven hours of canoeing, we approached the dike as the tide was coming in. The weather seemed to be threatening rain, and we saw no dry land anywhere. We had to push on in order to make our destination by dark. As we paddled toward the ocean we paddled much *harder* than I've ever paddled before. We were paddling against the incoming tide and blisters began to hurt. It was very difficult because we seemed to make very little progress. It took us forever to paddle just the half mile out to the coast.

Once we were out along the coast, we had only about a mile to paddle to our campsite. Our arms were tired, our legs were cramped, and our feet were wet. We made it, and again we knew God was faithful to those who trust Him.

"Have I not commanded you? Be strong and courageous. Do not be terrified; do not be discouraged, for the Lord your God will be with you wherever you go." – Joshua 1:9

Mark and his friend were in the lead canoe the entire way. Of course by the time Jim and I approached the shore (we were the last canoe), Mark had already beached his canoe. Living up to his reputation, Mark had again shinnied up another palm tree, cut down four or five coconuts, and was splitting them open. Unknown to us, he had hidden a machete in his canoe. He was ecstatic and we were not. What could have happened to Mark in a tree with a machete in hand? We were seven hours from civilization with no phone or means of making the trip back any different than the way we had come – no short cut.

We questioned, "What if he would have cut his hand or his foot?" We were certainly not equipped for an accident like that. Here we were camping out along the coast. Our small group of thirteen people was alone, with nothing but the ocean all around us. It was like living on Gilligan's Island – an experience unlike any of us had ever had before. We beached our canoes, set up our tents, and began to fix our dinner meal. But, we failed to anticipate the tide coming in and out and almost lost our canoes that evening.

The next day was beautiful, warm, and sunny. We were on our own private shell beach and blessed with our own supply of coconuts. Every night raccoons invaded our site and stole all the Christmas candy the kids had in their back packs. Everyone claimed that the coons even unzipped the pockets of their packs to get the candy. I'm not sure about a coon's ability to handle a zipper, but the candy was gone.

To fill the evenings, the kids came up with a game like football they called "Kill Ball". It soon became apparent that if anyone tackled you and you fell into yucca plants, you were dead meat. It was very hazardous as the dangerously spiked yucca plants were everywhere, especially the ones that bordered their makeshift football field. Every now and then we'd hear this horrible scream as someone landed on top of the "killer plants". Our campers had a great time, and it was a tremendous experience with memories for a lifetime. We certainly laughed a lot!

When the tide went out, we could explore the beach and all the little creatures the ocean left behind. Of course Mark caught the largest horseshoe crab. He never was interested in simple things like shells.

We spent three days on the coast before our adventurous group packed everything in the canoes and paddled back to Flamingo. We left in the early morning, and our short half- mile trip in saltwater was again very difficult since the tide was going the opposite direction we were. I remember looking over my right shoulder at a palm tree on the shore to gage our progress. There wasn't any! It seemed like we were standing still and not moving at all. Eventually we made it to the dike and portaged back into fresh water for the remainder of the seven-hour trip back to Flamingo.

Our Florida Christmas break trip culminated at Disney World. It was New Year's Eve, and our youth pastor led us in worship and served communion to us in the bus. The devotions for the trip were based on the Ornaments of Christianity and How Do We Wear Them? We discussed self-acceptance, acceptance of others, humility, peace, convictions, freedom, and love. We thought about our lives and how we could honor God more with our actions. We were grateful for the openness and honesty of the young people as they shared with us.

There had been some personality problems with some of the teens on the trip. So this special time in the Word helped clear some of our growing tension and redirect their attitudes as well as their lives. We began to see their hearts open up. God was so faithful, and many of our teens learned to ask forgiveness. Healing in our group was restored.

We did not plan to go into Disney on New Year's Eve, so we waited until New Year's Day. This trip was so full of challenge, excitement, fun, and special times with the Lord. Everyone was filled with memories that have certainly lasted a lifetime. It was a trip where we saw what God would do when we allow Him to demonstrate His love, His care, and His blessings.

Our travel trip home was uneventful, and the young adventurers went back to school with stories that very few could top.

The Tapestry of Five Pines was beginning to take shape, but the Everglades Trip was only the beginning. The 1980 Christmas break trip weaved very colorful strands in and out of our Tapestry. There was excitement, challenge, prayer and trust, ministry, community building with our youth, and many lessons learned for everyone – especially Jim and me. I learned to trust God in new experiences. The John 10:10 passage spoke of the abundant life, and thirteen people experienced a sample of that.

ꙮ ꙮ ꙮ ꙮ ꙮ ꙮ ꙮ

First Backpacking Trip: Porcupine Mountains – 1981
"You will go out in joy and be lead forth in peace; the mountains and hills will burst into song before you, and all the trees of the field will clap their hands." –
Isaiah 55:12

Richard Roach's enthusiasm for wilderness adventure immediately got us involved in our first backpacking trip. Our first group consisted of: Mark and his father, Dr. Roach, Jim, and a number of other teens. They headed to the Porcupine Mountains in the upper peninsula (U.P.) of Michigan for a week-long backpacking trip.

Days before the trip, Dr. Roach asked the team members to meet at our house to learn how to pack the food and their backpacks. Everyone had their packs in the living room except Mark. He had his pack standing around the corner in the hall. Richard clearly explained the limited needs for the trip and how to pack. But as we found out later, Mark decided that he might need more food and more equipment than what Richard suggested; even an extra pair of hiking boots!

After a long drive to the U.P., our adventurous group proceeded to get their gear out. Our hikers entered the park and headed to the trailhead at the southwest corner of the Porcupine Mountains Wilderness State Park. They needed to work in a buddy system to help the other person get their backpack on. When it came time for someone to help Mark get his pack on, they realized that it was almost impossible to lift up. His pack took *two* people to lift it and place it on Mark's shoulders, but he said he could handle it.

Besides Mark's extra gear, he was very willing to carry more than his share of the group's equipment such as tents, cookware, and of course the food packs. Now don't get me wrong. Mark was physically capable to carry a heavier load, but he was a *wee bit* bent over as the group headed out.

At the beginning of the hike, the group missed the trailhead and started out on the beach of Lake Superior. They had to climb a sand dune in order to get back on the trail. "The climb" did Mark in, and some of his eighty-plus pound pack was immediately distributed to other people – especially the second pair of hiking boots! His dad volunteered to carry them. Oh, the lessons they began to learn.

Dr. Roach used his wonderful ability to apply Scripture applications to almost any life-time situations, and God began to fulfill our vision of challenge in the ministry of wilderness trips. The girls who gave us the impression of being very "tough" that first day of hiking, ended up being very fragile. The trails and the difficult terrain began to wear on them. The week-long trip was one of the most difficult things they had ever done. But, as it turned out, they signed up and participated in every event Five Pines offered from then on.

The month of June came, and Kelly went into the Air Force. We continued to pray for her and others who had experienced these life-changing moments. We couldn't help but wonder what other life-changing programs God had planned for Five Pines.

ELEVEN

A Vision Realized
"The Yellow Straw Trail"

THAT SAME YEAR, we initiated a larger outreach into area churches by doing hayrides for youth groups. Soon our fall hayrides became a favorite activity for many local youth pastors. Jim acquired permission from the farmer to the west of our land to use his 140 acres to provide a longer hayride time. It also offered our participants more of the beautiful colors of a Michigan autumn and a safer ride by staying off country roads. There had been some recent fatal accidents in the state of Michigan by other groups who ran hayrides on roads with unmarked wagons. At one point, we were the only organization in the State of Michigan that could obtain insurance for a hayride program.

Jim maintained the wagons and tractors with every aspect of safety in mind. He built up the sides of the wagons about two feet high. Jim always filled each wagon with about six bales of loose straw where most other people just used unopened bales. This meant that many years we went through 120 to 130 bales of straw. Our strictly-observed rules included no standing up during the ride and no jumping off. Safety first. Some of our participants got a little "exuberant" in throwing the straw, and hay rides sometimes came back with literally bare wagons. A new tractor driver never got lost because of the "yellow straw trail" marked by previous hayrides.

Our tractors pulled the wagons full of twenty people through open fields, wooded areas, and up and down some steep hills and deep gullies. We offered the best and safest hayrides in the area, and Jim's attempts at constantly improving what we offered groups paid off. Five years later we were running 1,500 people, and just three years after that the numbers *doubled*. In 1989 we ran 3,000 people on fall hayrides.

We added more benches around the Maple Glen Fire Circle and eventually added two more fire circles so that we could do multiple groups at one time. In addition to youth groups, we were doing young couples groups, physically and mentally disabled groups, and people of every age. Some weekends we began hayrides on Saturday at 11:00 a.m. and ran them every hour with the last one going out at 9:00 p.m.

Many times one group would be singing praise songs in one pit, and a totally different church group would join in from another pit. We created the fire pits to be a distance apart, but their like faith brought them close together. I loved being out in the night with the smell of a campfire and the joy of people having such a good time.

We never envisioned in 1977 that the Maple Glen fire circle (plus two others) would be used by thousands and thousands of people. For over thirty-five years, our guests have enjoyed a night under the stars, roasting marshmallows and hot dogs, and singing praise songs to our Creator. More importantly, hundreds of young people have given their lives to the Lord for the first time around a glowing fire in the dark of the night. God has richly blessed Jim in his efforts (and fulfilled a vision) to have people enjoy this land of his ancestors.

We had more than our share of both humorous and difficult times in all these years of hayrides. In the early days, we were doing an afternoon hayride for a group of Girl Scout Brownies. Kirk was in high school at the time and was one of the drivers. He was to check all of the wagons and gas up the tractors. They loaded up the Brownies and excitedly started out. The weather didn't look promising, but they would be back before the storm would hit. After a while, though, I didn't hear the tractors coming back and began to worry – and of course pray. That always seemed to be my job back at the fire pit as I readied the fire.

The storm clouds were forming fast over Lake Michigan, and I knew the length of good weather was short. Finally Kirk came walking across the field. He had not checked the gas gauge and ran out of gas way over on the other farmland. Not far behind him was a lady with one of the little girls. She was allergic to the straw and suffering from an asthma attack. My response was, "Why would her mother let her come on a hay ride if she was allergic to the straw?" The lady said, "I am her mother."

Well, Kirk proceeded to get some gas for the tractor and rescue the other scouts. By the time he and the wagon got back to Five Pines, it was not only raining but turning to sleet. All the Brownies were safe but a little wet. There again, one very important lesson was learned: Always check the gas tank.

Another time we had all three wagons out together. As they traveled out on our neighboring farmland, some people in the one wagon said, "Look at that wheel rolling across the field!" Sure enough, there was a wheel rolling right down the field toward the wooded area. They all laughed until they looked over the side of the wagon. It was from *their* wagon, and they were riding on only three wheels. Oops!

We didn't like starting a hayride as late as 9:00 at night, but we often did hayrides for groups from Indiana on CST (an hour behind us in Michigan). One night Jim, a dear friend and volunteer who drove more than his share of hayrides, left on the late run with a group of senior singles.

Five Pines has many natural springs running through its property, and they are on one of the lower areas on the trail. It had been a raining all week, and that weekend we ran numerous groups. The trail became very muddy, and the ruts in the road became deeper with each ride. Jim had driven the majority of the ride and was just re-entering Five Pines property. The wagon was loaded because some of the participants were rather large in size. As Jim attempted to pull the wagon up a hill, the wheels sank deeper and deeper. Soon the mud was up to the axles.

The message that came across the radio I held in my hand was, "Bring lanterns. We need to walk the entire group of people out." The cold night mist had begun to settle across the open lowland of the field in the back. The moon was bright and our group of senior singles carefully trekked through the field and back down the trail to the Activity Center. Everyone made it safely, but I don't believe that group ever came back! An early afternoon hayride would have been best.

The thirty years of doing hayrides was one of the best times in our lives. Jim absolutely loved the people. Everyone had such a great time. I loved working with the different groups, but I thoroughly enjoyed the night-time adventures.

We offered the half-hour hayrides and then an hour at a fire pit (and we started the fire for them). The groups brought their own refreshments. It was usually hot dogs, chips, marshmallows, and drinks. My job was to make sure their food got down to the table at the fire pit, and I would start the fire and keep it going until the wagons got back. I cannot venture to say how many fires I have started in my life.

One night, early in our ministry, when our program director, Nancy and I were sitting down at the Maple Glen Fire Circle, she called to an owl in the nearby big maple tree. It was a great experience to hear it answer her call and move from tree to tree as it investigated these two weird people.

Many groups had one or more people stay back at the fire pit instead of going on the hayride. One evening, a lady stayed and we began talking. She asked me how long we had been doing hayrides and if I worked at Five Pines. As always, this opened a door to tell The Story. She was amazed at how God had worked in our lives and the doors He opened for us.

As the evening drew to a close and the group was leaving, there was a knock at our door. The lady I had talked to handed Jim an envelope containing sixty-one one dollar bills. This was the amount she had collected from the group for the hayride, but she had already written a check to cover the event. She was so touched by our story that she wanted to give the collected amount of money to Jim and me as well.

I love being out at night because the night-time sky speaks to me of God's majesty. *"The heavens declare the glory of God; the skies proclaim the work of his hands"* (Psalm 19:1). Sitting there at the fire pit, I have probably sung more songs of praise and spoken more conversations with the Lord than at any time in my life. So many memories of those quiet times with God. I've been so blessed.

Memories of those nights allow me to add the oranges, reds, and browns from the autumn leaves to the Tapestry. God also adds the threads of the colors of the deep darkness of the night-time sky and the harvest moon as it rises over the horizon in the east – and the peace it seems to bring to one's soul.

In 1981 we did hayrides for about 350 people and by 1992 we drew over 3,000 people to the fast-growing popularity of a fall hayride. It was a stepping-stone program which introduced people, many for the first time, to a rather new ministry in Berrien Center, Michigan, called Five Pines – and hayrides are still a big fall activity to this day.

TWELVE

The Land to Five Pines

"No eye has seen, no ear has heard, no mind has conceived what God has prepared for those who love him." – 1 Corinthians 2:9

THE ABOVE PASSAGE is a portion of Isaiah 64:4 which the Apostle Paul quoted. The Isaiah verse ends with *"...who acts on behalf of those who wait on Him."* In 1981 Jim was convinced that he needed to let go of the thirty-three acres of his family farm to the ministry of Five Pines Christian Family Center. The Scofield family would retain the original house and the two acres it was built on. This again was a huge release of something that Jim's family had so valued and faithfully held onto for over 140 years. It was their heritage, but Jim felt that God wanted all of what we were. That meant the land that had been cleared and farmed for so many generations of his family.

We had been learning over and over to let go and let God and now was the time to let the Lord have the farm. He had a plan for this land. We would trust Him and pray that we would not look back. We can't always know it is the right time, but if we believe in our hearts that everything belongs to God anyway, why do we hesitate when we doubt the timing? The land belonged to God much earlier than it did to the five generations of Jim's mother's family through the Murphy line.

One year after we donated the land to the ministry, we learned that many of our neighbors could not figure out what Jim was doing. The talk circulated through the township that all Jim wanted to do was get the land off of the tax records. In reality, Five Pines continued to pay the township taxes for the first ten years of ministry, even though we didn't have to. Jim's decision to pay the taxes demonstrated who he was and the respect he had gained with the township board as this new non-profit organization began to grow.

Then one day our township supervisor came over to our house and asked Jim why we were still paying the taxes when Five Pines was tax-exempt. Jim told him that he felt we would still pay the taxes as long as we had the money. He said that as we built more buildings the taxes would increase. He advised Jim to take advantage of the tax deduction granted to us as a non-profit organization – and we did.

ଥ ଥ ଥ ଥ ଥ ଥ ଥ

A Most Important Thread in Our Tapestry
"There is a friend that sticks closer than a brother." – Proverbs 18:24b

After we became believers, someone in our church was interested in a lot on our property, but the perk test on the well came up negative. For the second time the sale didn't go through. (The first time was the pool-for-parcel-of-land exchange that fell through.)

A third attempt to sell the lot on the west border of the property happened when God informed us of an ideal situation. A former pastor was working on his doctorate and in need of a lot to build a home on. This time the perk test was okay, and the pastor applied for a loan. God had indeed held this lot for this particular couple. They became very important threads in our ministry and especially in our private lives.

God had an important reason to save that lot for them and knew, way in advance, of our need for accountability partners. Eventually David & Alice Maysick became our best friends and certainly mentors for life. They are willing to pray for us and have open ears when Jim and Judy needed someone to talk to.

It has been an enjoyable place to live for David and Alice. They have enjoyed watching the people come and go during all four seasons of activity fun at Five Pines. The deer have a four-lane highway across their yard, and the raccoons seem to enjoy the bird food in their bird feeders.

God prepared this property for a special couple who have

meant so much to Jim and me. I'm not sure we could have made it through the ups and downs over the years, if it had not been for the faithfulness of David and Alice Maysick. They have supported us closer than a brother. Their threads are woven in and out of this Tapestry of Five Pines so many times and for so many different reasons. We have been blessed!

THIRTEEN

A Visionary Sent by God – A Golden Thread

"This is what the Lord says, he who made the earth, the Lord who formed it and established it – the Lord is his name: 'Call to me and I will answer you and tell you great and unsearchable things you do not know.'" – Jeremiah 33:2-3

HARV CHROUSER WAS A DYNAMIC MAN – and a great coach. Don Gast, one of our original board members, played football for him when he was a student at Wheaton College. Later on Harv began Honeyrock, Wheaton College's outward bound camp in Wisconsin. Honeyrock was one of the first Christian camps in the nation and was known around the nation for its magnificent wilderness program. Harv's wife, Dot, was director of the girl's camp and both were well known in Christian circles.

Don was a visionary and thought it would be good if Harv could stop by sometime and evaluate our land and facilities. He could give us some ideas of what we could do with this run-down piece of property and especially the dilapidated barn. Little did we know that Harv Chrouser's visit would be a life-changing experience, not only to Jim and me but to the land Jim's ancestors had lived on and farmed for so many years.

One Saturday morning in the spring of 1981, Harv drove up in our driveway. This was our first meeting, and he was a "man on a mission" from the time he stepped out of his car. Harv was always a man on a mission who helped Christian camps all over the nation. He never even stopped at the house, but immediately walked over to our run-down barn. One could tell by the determined steps he took that his mind was going a thousand thoughts a minute. He was a man who left absolutely no dust under his feet and no detail uncovered. He entered

68

the old barn, and Jim and I caught up with him there and introduced ourselves.

Not a moment was wasted as he related what we should do to the barn and how to do it. He advised us to decide if we wanted to keep the original interior and resurface the outside or remodel the inside and have it look like the old barn on the outside. Harv was indeed an exciting man, talking a mile-a-minute with tons of ideas.

Listening to Harv was like drinking in a wonderful cup of hot chocolate on a cold, blustery winter day. He warmed our hearts with thoughts of all kinds of possibilities. He was such a character but also so knowledgeable and full of so much enthusiasm. Ideas just popped off the top of his head, and we were overwhelmed with excitement.

Harv said that if we remodeled the old barn, it would be very unique and be a drawing place for this ministry. It would leave an impression on people's minds, and they would want to return. Teens would see it as a place to hang-out; a "warm feeling" building, not threatening to the un-churched young people with whom we had hoped to share Christ. Harv told us he knew teens would love it, and that was exactly what we wanted to hear.

He later walked the thirty-three acres of our land and shared with us a whole array of things we could do. "You could easily have a camp for kids," he said. Harv reminded us that the size of the acreage didn't matter – God could use anything. What a positive thinker! What a salesman for Christian camping! What a gift from God! Harv and his visions truly became a prominent thread in the Tapestry of Five Pines.

Later we learned the huge impact that Harv Chrouser had made not only on Five Pines but on many people and camps around the country. Harv was truly a giant of the faith and a giant in Christian camping. We were blessed to have his enthusiasm woven into our hearts that Saturday morning.

Before he left that day he told us, "You need to start a day camp."

My heart sank as I said, "Oh no, Harv, you don't understand. We are comfortable working with young people, *teens* – not younger children. What in the world would we do with them?"

We could not *imagine* doing programming for little kids. Harv tried to encourage us by saying it would be very simple. Have their parents bring them out or take the bus into town to pick them up. Have them bring their own lunch and just stir up a jug of "bug juice". He told us to teach a Bible class each morning and take them on a nature hike in the woods. Let them swim in the pool (our own 20-foot by 40-foot pool) and do a craft class. In the afternoon we could play group games and have a free swim.

Well this may have sounded easy to some people but not to us; *teens were our ministry!* We said no to Harv again. He wisely said that it was important to share Christ with the younger children, and then they would be "seed" for our other programs like the wilderness trips and day camp counselors.

We were forgetting that this was God's ministry, and God could do *anything*. The Apostle Paul stated in 2 Timothy 4:17: *"But the Lord stood at my side and gave me strength, so that through me the message might be fully proclaimed ..."*

We needed to be reminded that Jesus said, *"What is impossible with men is possible with God"* (Luke 18:27). We were no longer living a performance-driven life, and it didn't matter what WE could do. It mattered what GOD could do through us. In the beginning we stepped out in faith, and this needed to continue to be a faith-based ministry in every aspect of Five Pines.

Well, we were excited about Harv's encouragement about the barn. He had left us with many dreams and much hope. Harv was a very substantial golden thread woven in and out of the Tapestry. God had blessed us and demonstrated He was with us.

Both Don Gast and Harv Chrouser were people who so have impacted our lives and this ministry. The two of them had become the major threads that God used to weave Five Pines Ministries into the beautiful Tapestry it has become. Five Pines would become a ministry whose sole purpose is to share Christ and His redemptive work with all who step through our doors or onto our property.

FOURTEEN

Initial Step of Faith – The 1850 Barn Project

"Honor the Lord with your wealth, with first fruits of all your crops; then your barns will be filled to overflowing." - Proverbs 3:9

AS OUR MINISTRY OUTREACH began to grow, we decided to get serious about some kind of facility. Kirk introduced us to cross-country skiing and cut some trails through our property. We only had a few sets of skis and boots, but it was a beginning.

One Sunday after church, in 1982, Dr. Roach and Priscilla invited some people over to our house to ski. It was a beautiful day with new-fallen snow, and Richard was excited to teach some of his friends how to ski. Being raised in northern Minnesota, he was also an avid skier. There were two problems:

1. We were out of town for the weekend, and there was no one at our home.

2. We didn't have any buildings to store our few sets of skis. The few sets we had were stored in Jim's parent's mobile home while they were in Florida for the winter.

Richard and Priscilla invited *lots* of people – and they all came. We arrived home from my parent's home in Warsaw, Indiana, about 4:00 in the afternoon. As we approached our home we thought, "What is going on?" We couldn't get in our car-packed driveway. In fact as we opened the back door, suitcases in hand, we could hardly step into the kitchen. Priscilla had hot chocolate on the stove, people were everywhere in the house, and they were all having a great time!

This proved one important thing: We needed a building of some sort – and soon.

We had talked to a few contractors about restoring the old barn and putting kids in it instead of horses. But each one told us the same thing: "Tear it down and put up a pole barn." Granted, our horses had as much snow on their backs when they were *in* the barn as when they were *outside*. The exterior siding and roof were in deplorable shape. Many of the sagging floorboards were missing. It looked like a hopeless project.

But each time we stepped into that old barn and looked at the huge wooden pegged beams and the beauty of the massive structure, we knew in our hearts we didn't want to tear it down. We remembered Harv Chrouser's words as well: "This barn will be very unique and be a drawing place for this ministry. It will leave an impression on people's minds, and they will want to return."

There was so much history in it, and it meant so much to our family because it was part of Jim's family heritage. Jim had worked and played in it. Our two children had spent endless hours with their horses in the barn and babied thirteen kittens in the loft at one time. We all loved the smell of that old building and wanted to save it and hopefully rebuild it.

A few years earlier we had purchased another old barn in Berrien Springs for $50 with the plans of tearing it down and building it back up. But it took us a year to tear it down, and the owners were getting a little anxious because of the time it was taking. We were doing it piece-by-piece and marking each piece because we wanted to restore it – but it seemed hopeless. Finally we took a chainsaw and cut the main beams and let the whole barn fall! We brought back all the salvageable wood and stored it outside and covered it with a tarp.

ख ख ख ख ख ख

Barn Transformation Begins – 1982

"And the vessel that he made of clay was marred in the hand of the potter; so he made it again into another vessel, as it seemed good to the potter to make." – Jeremiah 18:4 NKJV

A massive undertaking began during the summer of 1982. The only part of the barn that was salvageable and sturdy was the huge beam structure – the remainder of the barn went downhill from there. It would need a new foundation, and that meant all the huge boulders in its present foundation needed to be dug out and removed. A cement block foundation would replace the old boulder foundation before we could pour a cement floor. The "massive" in this job was the boulders.

Ed Banish and his family worked diligently on the foundation all summer. They dug out the huge boulders and built up a cement block foundation. His daughter Linda, used every ounce of strength in her young body to dig out the old cement floor (originally the box stall for horses). It wasn't an easy job, but this energetic family was so faithful in completing this daunting task. God miraculously brought these people into our lives.

We needed to address the roof at the same time. Jim and a number of board members proceeded to attack that project. The pitch of the barn roof was very steep, and it was a harrowing task for these amateurs. The old roof had to be removed, and all of the sheeting had to be replaced.

The angels were there protecting our crew of volunteers. Bill Wurzel, a board member, fell off the roof right down into the ditch where all the huge boulders were dug out to build the new foundation. Rocks and cement blocks were everywhere. It was truly a miracle that Bill wasn't severely injured or killed. Bill also spent many an hour on building maintenance, especially electrical work. The work went on with all volunteer labor – a labor of love to fulfill a vision from God.

The weather around the holidays was unseasonably warm, with temperatures in the high 50's. On Christmas Eve day, 1982, Jim was able to pour the floor in the kitchen portion of the barn (the section that used to be the box stall).

The main "floor" of the old barn was wooden planking two inches by fourteen inches. Much of the planking was missing or broken, and all had to be removed and fill dirt added before Jim could pour the cement. As spring approached, the entire floor of the old barn was poured, one load of cement at a time from our small cement mixer on the back of Jim's old Ford tractor.

Kirk and a few other young men were willing to help with this very time-consuming project. The floor measured thirty feet by thirty-three feet (close to 1,000 square feet with kitchen section included). Jim and his crew were only able to pour an eight-foot by eight-foot square (one bag of cement) at a time. Jim felt blessed that we had the cement mixer and was extremely pleased and proud when the floor was completed.

Harv had also suggested that we build an overhang roof across the front of the barn where the big front doors were, enclose it, and build our main entrance there. Eventually there was a door facing east and one facing west when it was enclosed.

By July of 1983, the barn floor and overhang entrance was partially completed, enough for us to host a wedding reception for Tanya and her fiancé Jerry Waddington. This was exciting because a lot of hard work was paying off. The bridal party's head table was out on the new front porch of the barn and the buffet tables inside. This was a big step, and we were beginning to see a dream come true.

As winter approached, we knew it would be important to hire a contractor to side the outer walls. But first we needed to address the insulation problems. Since we chose to leave the inner structure of the old barn exposed and resurface the outside walls with siding, we researched the type of insulation that was needed. Harv had suggested that we buy two-inch refrigeration insulation and apply it over the outside siding and then re-side it.

Once again, our dear board member Don Gast stepped in. Don had a general knowledge of construction and *many* connections in the business world. Don's favorite saying was, "I know someone who owes me a favor." Because Don had done so much for so many people in the twin cities of St. Joseph and Benton Harbor, there were literally hundreds of people who were willing to help him out!

Don had a friend in the insulation business. He did not manufacture the two-inch refrigeration insulation that we needed, but he was willing to do Don a favor. He shipped from another supplier a semi-load of the insulation to fully cover the entire exterior of the barn.

We never met this wonderful generous man, and we never received a bill for the insulation!

One year later, we felt we needed to insulate the ceiling. We received another semi-load of enough insulation to install four inches in the ceiling of this massive barn. Our "old barn" or activity center was now ready to be heated and offer a toasty unique place for people to enjoy. Harv said the completed barn would be a showplace for the ministry, and it was – and still is today.

As the exterior barn work continued, Nancy Poling, a volunteer with our youth ministry and just out of high school, helped me with some inside work. We covered some of the walls with the weathered siding we had removed from the other old barn we took down. The red-stained weathered siding ended up being a real bonus to finish off the walls and added to the rugged décor. God had given us provisions for the interior of the Activity Center before we even envisioned it.

I remember the men who were putting on the exterior siding looking at Nancy and me as if we were crazy. We were two amateur women carpenters measuring, sawing, and nailing all this siding to the inside walls. We installed the barn wood at an angle, in a pattern, and straight across. It ended up looking very good, added to the class of an old barn, and still looks good thirty years later! Since I'd always been interested in interior decorating, I had a great time being an interior barn decorator.

We had many antiques lying around in the original barn, in our attic and our basement, so it was easy to make the interior look really "old barn". There were saws, signs, all kinds of old tools, shovels, scales, crocks, and buckets. The decor worked so well, and it was all free of cost. Sometime during the initial remodeling of the barn, I stopped at a small junk store with all kinds of items for resale. I had never stopped there before, but for some odd reason I was curious and went in. God was again leading and providing.

As soon as I walked in the door, there on the table before me were two very large black wrought iron chandeliers. They were about forty-two inches in diameter and had twenty candle-like light fixtures.

How perfect they would be hanging in the main two-story part of the barn! But could I afford them? When I asked the price, it didn't take long to get them in the back of my van and excitedly drive back home and show Jim. The price was right – $15 apiece. The Lord continued to provide for this remodeling adventure we had stepped out in faith to do.

God was doing a mighty work in our lives. There were many people who doubted what the Scofields' were doing with that old barn. A year previous to the re-construction, we had built a new pole barn to the east of our house for our horses, and now we were remodeling the old barn to house teenagers! A lot of our neighbors thought we were crazy, but God had given Jim a vision of a ministry to young people and a strong faith. God used Harv Chrouser and other people who believed that, if God gave you a desire, He would graciously fulfill that desire. We had "stepped out of the boat" and were trusting in God for all things. We certainly saw His mighty hand upon this endeavor.

For our next step we went to Dale and Norma Weldy, a couple who truly lived Jesus' message that *"it is more blessed to give than to receive"* (Acts 20:35). Initially, we heated the ole barn with a small wood-burner that we placed in the northwest corner. But eventually Jim ordered a large wood-burning furnace with ductwork from Weldy Sales. The furnace did a much better job of heating the large building, but we still kept the small wood-burner to give a cozy effect during the winter.

Months after installing the large furnace, we realized that Weldy's had never sent us a bill for the furnace. Jim drove out to their store to pay for it, and Dale said he and his wife had decided not send a bill to Five Pines – the furnace was a gift. God had His people in places to accomplish His mission.

The Weldy's were important colorful threads that God had also woven in and out of the Tapestry throughout the thirty-five years of Five Pines Ministries. They lived their lives faithful to their Lord and continued to bless not only this ministry but others. They rejoiced in giving gifts time and time again. What a privilege to be partakers of their generosity.

Here's a little back-story to how God orchestrated this gift of a furnace. The Weldy's became involved in the early ministry of Five Pines through a difficult young people's canoe trip. Some years earlier, we offered weekend canoe trips to Turkey Run State Park in southern Indiana. Dale was a youth leader at his church and had a "difficult" group of young boys in his youth group. He booked a weekend trip with Five Pines to Turkey Run but was adamant he wasn't going. He confessed, "These guys are too rough for me!"

So we sent our son Kirk and Nancy Poling to staff the trip. Low and behold Dale's evaluation proved to be right on. These boys were a challenge to our staff! The group attempted to burn up a picnic table at the state park. They also threw firecrackers into the restrooms and caused all kinds of trouble on the trip. Dale said any ministry that would take on that group was worthy of his support!

Dale and Norma were by far some of the most supportive, generous and active people throughout the thirty-five years of our ministry. Dale faithfully cooked our pork for our annual Golf Outing/Pig Roasts in September each year. Dale also equipped us with our first golf cart when he saw us running all over these thirty-plus acres and learned we didn't have a cart. Just think – it all started with a difficult group of kids on a canoe trip.

FIFTEEN

Completion and Dedication of the Centerpiece

"He has made everything beautiful in its time." – Ecclesiastes 3:11

AS THE BARN PROJECT PROGRESSED, we needed carpeting on the floor. At first we just used odd pieces of carpet to cover the cement floor. Eventually, we received enough used carpeting (torn out of a large business) for the entire main floor. In fact it wears like steel since it still is there today. We also installed used windows, game tables, sofas, and tables' people had donated.

The wood furnace worked very efficiently and had served us well. As the years progressed, one of our very faithful supporters of the ministry, Mark Wurzel, blessed Five Pines with a wonderful Water Furnace geothermal system to replace the wood furnace. The new furnace was indeed a blessing because it provided us wonderful heat in the winter *and* air conditioning in the summer.

The sixty Steelcase chairs that have been in the Activity Center since the late 1980's were donated by a gentleman our teens befriended at the youth conference in Grand Rapids. He was going through a divorce, and our students shared with him their lunch and also about the ministry. They invited him to come to Five Pines sometime – and he did. He worked at Steelcase, and he would bring ten chairs each time he came. He brought his son to a few of our all-night New Year's Eve Celebrations. Our teens shared Jesus and he shared 60 chairs.

The first phase of the barn (Activity Center) remodel had cost us just $10,000 as work finished up in 1984. The Weldy gift of the wood burning furnace enabled Five Pines to heat the entire Activity Center with wood for the first ten years at almost no cost to the ministry.

ℬ ℬ ℬ ℬ ℬ ℬ ℬ

Four Men With Hammers

The original barn had only one loft on the east side and the west side was wide open two stories up. We discussed how much we liked the effect of the open ceiling on the west side. We also thought that another loft would enable us to have two game lofts and keep the main floor open for sofas and tables (and still not ruin the effect of the barn).

A very generous contractor from a local town, mentioned to us one night, "If you can get four men with hammers, I have the wood for the beams. In two nights we can build the west loft and the stairs up to it." We weren't sure if we wanted to add the second loft, but once it was done it fit the building and enhanced the use of it. It held our large pool table, a sofa, and a foosball table. God had indeed blessed.

This contractor and his wife became important threads God wove into the ministry. They and their children were involved in our ministry all through their high school years. Now their grandchildren are involved at Five Pines as well. Connecting with the different people who helped bring this ministry together was such an overwhelming experience and blessing. It was just as Harv had anticipated. God was indeed faithful to Jim and me as we learned to let go and watch the marvelous work of God in bringing together the ministry of Five Pines.

ℬ ℬ ℬ ℬ ℬ ℬ ℬ

Dedication of the Harv Chrouser Activity Center – 1985

In 1985, we dedicated the renovated Activity Center in Harv Chrouser's name. Our board of directors held a dedication dinner, and Harv and Dot were invited. He was by far the tool that God used to help us see the possibility of what the old barn could become. Harv had the gift of being a visionary, and God spoke through him in a mighty way.

The Chrousers stayed the night at our house. The next morning as we prepared to go to church, we realized there was something desperately wrong with Harv. He had had a stroke. We rushed him to Berrien General Hospital and called Don Gast (the administrator of Southwestern Medical Clinic). The clinic had many doctors on staff who knew Harv because they had graduated from Wheaton College when Harv was there.

Harv was in the hospital for about a week, and during that time he received hundreds of notes and calls of encouragement from leaders in the Christian community worldwide: Bill Bright, Billy Graham, and many more. Little did we realize how well-known and loved this man was in the eyes of so very many Christian people and leaders of our faith. God had blessed our little camp with Harv Chrouser, indeed a giant and a very major thread in our Tapestry.

Harv went on to encourage many camps across the nation as he did Five Pines, never stopping even as age began to take its toll. We figured that when the Lord came to take Harv home, God would probably find him on a bulldozer working at a camp somewhere. He went home to be with the Lord on April 21, 2002. Harv was in his eighties.

ℑ ℑ ℑ ℑ ℑ ℑ ℑ

Additions to Activity Center

The ministry continued to grow, and in 1987 we built an addition to the back section of the barn. A few years later we enclosed the space in between the ski room and the furnace room for an office. Wow, we even had an office and our first computer!

A gracious person from Whirlpool arranged for a donation of an entire room of kitchen cabinets from one of Whirlpool's display kitchens. (This wonderful gift came to us after we had spent much time with his teenage daughter trying to help her with some life issues.) A refrigerator was also donated, a pizza company donated pizza ovens, a large cooler came with the purchase of soft drinks, and we bought a hot dog roaster. We were in big business!

By 1990 Jim had decided to move the entrance of the Activity Center to the west side of the building. Our new entrance was a great addition, welcoming our guests with a small foyer and double doors to better accommodate the increasing participants in our programs. In 1995, one hundred and ninety-two people came together to praise the Lord in a ten-year celebration banquet of Five Pines in the Harv Chrouser Activity Center.

SIXTEEN

Boundary Water Canoe Trips

"And God said, 'Let the water teem with living creatures, and let birds fly above the earth across the expanse of the sky'... And God saw that it was good." –
Genesis 1:20-21

IN 1982 WE ADDED Dr. Richard Roach to our Board of Directors. Dr. Roach guided our first wilderness trip to the Porcupine Mountains, and he immediately encouraged Jim to plan our first week-long Boundary Water canoe trip. The absolutely beautiful pristine waterways of the Boundary Waters Canoe Area Wilderness (BWCAW) in northern Minnesota offered the challenge, excitement, and solitude away from everyday life that Jim had so envisioned. The 1,200 miles of canoe routes offered hundreds of different challenges in this unspoiled world-famous waterway.

In each trip, participants could experience a different series of lakes, some as long as five miles and others opening into smaller rivers. Our canoers enjoyed beautiful waterfalls, rock formations, and exciting wildlife like bald eagles, loons, moose, and black bear (sometimes as close as fifty yards!).

A day on the trail might consist of five or six portages with some as long as two miles. The rental canoe was equipped for a person to balance it on their shoulders and carry it across the portage. The challenge of portaging four canoes, the Duluth Packs, and all the gear numerous times a day always brought a good night's sleep – even if the pillow was a rock.

The Boundary Water trips became one of our most popular programs. The BWCAW had a limit of no more than ten people to a campsite, so most of our trips were kept to that number of participants. There were times when we had to offer a double trip due to the popularity. Five Pines has offered almost one trip a summer for the last twenty-eight years, and our office manager, Mike Emerson, holds the record of being on twenty of them. We also had area churches form their own trip and had staff from Five Pines outfit and guide it.

These experiences have produced stories and memories that last for a lifetime. Some groups have used their rain ponchos as sails to make use of the wind in order to cross Lake la Croix. At times the crossing could take all day without the wind. Campsites were rather rugged (especially in Canada) and consisted of nothing more than a fire pit and potty pit set back in the wooded area. Portages in Canada are not as well maintained as in the states, so missing a portage or getting lost were sometimes part of the stories from returning trip participants.

Early in our BWCAW trips, four adventurers traveled up to the Canadian waterways: Jim, Dr. Roach, Dave and Tom. It was early spring and very cold. The ice had gone out just two weeks previously, and they were in the most primitive areas of the Canadian portion of the Boundary waters. They were excited to be able to fish. Jim recalls catching some mighty nice Northern Pike which were big enough for them to eat all week. Dr. Roach used his storytelling talents to entertain the adventurous group with his harrowing experiences of the past.

All the drinking and cooking water had to be filtered, and most meals were dehydrated and just needed water and heat to prepare. We purchased a food dehydrator and became experts in packing three meals a day for five days for each trip camp. We prepared fourteen meals for each trip with directions on how to prepare the meals. Bottled spaghetti sauce and applesauce could easily be dehydrated into light-weight fruit "leather" which we packed in plastic bags for light packing. The campers then rehydrated these sauces with boiling water to bring them to their natural consistency. Spaghetti and applesauce became a favorite meal.

Lunch on the trail could be eaten in the canoe and was very simple: Rye Krisp crackers topped with cheese and summer sausage or peanut butter and jelly. Because we were prohibited from taking bottles or cans into the national preserve, we packed the peanut butter and jelly in plastic bags. We instructed our campers to cut one small hole in the corner of the plastic bag and then squeeze the peanut butter and jelly across each cracker as if you were decorating a cake. The plastic bags and brown bags the lunches were packed in were easy to pack out at the end of the week. We always added candy bars or granola bars as a later snack.

Breakfast was easy because of the instant cereals, granola bars, fruit leathers, and hot chocolate we could purchase ready to pack. Meals were simple, easy to pack in the large Duluth Packs, and yet nourishing. Even the meals were an adventure for first-time campers. It was unwise to let the campers bring extra food because each food pack had to be strung up in a tree at night so as not to draw bears.

But as in past trips, one of our early campers (and I'll not mention a name) was again known to "pack heavy" with those snacks he couldn't live without. I think he suffered from a fear of starving out in the wilderness. I recall once when I shared with a lady at work how I had to pack fourteen meals for ten people who were going on a wilderness trip. She said "Well, why don't you just tell them to get out of the canoes and go to McDonald's?" She had no idea what wilderness camping was all about, did she?

Five Pines wilderness trips inspired those special times of experiencing God – the beauty, the solitude, the simplicity of life. There were also the unplanned challenges that stirred our hearts to plead for God's intervention: unpredictable weather, getting lost on unmarked portages, canoes tipping with food packs falling overboard into the water (and a whole week of meals getting wet), or bears in your food pack in camp. On one trip a participant didn't take her medication and had serious mental problems. On another trip one of the staff leaders severely cut his foot and could not help on any of the portages. They had to improvise a makeshift crutch and tough it out through the week.

On one of our earlier Boundary Water trips, Kirk was in a canoe with Dr. Doug Taylor. Doug was an adventurous seventy-year-old retired missionary. He had been known to take some very challenging trips while in Africa, so this Boundary Water trip would be very mellow by his standards.

On one of the portages Kirk and Doug decided that they would not take the first of three portages available but try the second one closer to the falls. It was early spring and the water was high making the third portage too risky. Bold and adventuresome they were, until their canoe tipped over. Kirk popped up right away but no Dr. Taylor. Some time elapsed and still no Dr. Taylor! Where was Doug? Kirk's immediate thoughts were not positive. Then finally up pops Dr. Taylor way downstream with a big smile on his face. The two were able to reach a tiny island of land across from the first portage and Jerry and Dr. Roach were able to get them, their canoe, Duluth pack, and Kirk's camera. Soon they re-joined their group back on the first portage (the one they should have taken in the first place).

Kirk had become quite a photographer and valued his camera and all the photos he had taken prior to the camera's trip down the rapids. When he got back home, he sent it in to see if it was salvageable. The company dried it out but didn't guarantee it would work. It did and was still useable and took great photos years later.

On another trip, our group was on a waterway on the Canadian side of the Boundary Waters and was coming back over to the American side. It was to be a 150-mile training trip in five days, and Dr. Roach was leading and teaching. Many of the portages on the Canadian side were more primitive and not as well marked as on the American side.

Jerry Waddington, our son-in-law, was on a portage carrying a canoe on his shoulders. As he was carrying it and walking down the trail he broke through the bog falling completely under water and dropping the canoe to the side but since he continued to hold on to the canoe with one hand he was able to pull himself back up. Tanya was walking behind him; one minute he was in front of her and the next he was gone. It was not a muddy type of thing but a part of the lake that had growth over it, like a carpet, but was lake/water under it. There were mounds/clumps of trees/solid ground throughout so they put the packs in the canoes and slid the canoes across the bog and hopped from mound to mound the final 50 yards to the lake.

Praise the Lord for the canoe and God's hand of protection.

We also suffered some calamities on the long twelve-hour bus trip up to the outfitter in Ely, Minnesota. Twice the bus broke down. One time it was fixed, and the next time it had to be towed home (at a very expensive fee).

I received a call at church that Sunday morning with a plea: "Bring some vans and meet us on I-94 just south of Madison, Wisconsin." I immediately asked some people at church if they would let Five Pines borrow their vans and also drive them up with me to pick up the group. Camp buses are as notorious as church buses – always in need of repair.

Jerry, also led a number of Boundary Waters trips during the years that we offered two or more trips a summer. He also led two week-long bike trips to Mackinac, one in 1985 and again in 1986. The group averaged seven or eight bikers and a driver for the backup van. They biked about seventy-five miles a day, camped in state parks.

The wilderness trips have woven colorful threads throughout the Tapestry of Five Pines, including the vivid colors of the pristine waters, the colors of northern pine and birch woods, and the sounds of hundreds of loons. Over three hundred people have been on one or more of these Boundary Water trips: father/daughter, father/son, young people who served in other Five Pines programs, and men and women just needing to get away and spend time alone with the Creator of the universe.

Five Pines has offered and taken a Boundary Water trip almost every other year since its inception in 1982. Mike Emerson has played a major role in encouraging people to participate in this life-changing experience. It was indeed difficult to see this most rewarding experience come to an end.

We pray that these experiences will continue to speak to those who participated and that their lives will be forever changed because they encountered God through the serenity and solitude of His beautiful creation.

SEVENTEEN

The Vibrant Colors of Youth Programs

"Let us not become weary in doing good, for at the proper time we will reap a harvest if we do not give up." – Galatians 6:9

AS WE BEGAN TO REACH OUT to area youth and youth leaders, we sensed a need to bring youth from different churches together and offer a prom alternative. Many of our young people chose not to attend their high school prom because of the many un-chaperoned activities that were part of the events. Even some of the dancing was unfavorable to some churches. Five Pines could sponsor an all-night alternative that could still offer them an outstanding event.

Our first sponsored Non-Prom event was held in May of 1982 and brought 112 young people! It was a great success and the beginning of a number of years of all night prom alternatives.

We didn't have any buildings to hold such an event in, (our Activity Center wasn't completed until two years later) but we were told that a camp just a few miles from Five Pines had recently built a new dining hall. It was perfect for the catered dinner and entertainment portion of the evening.

For the second event of the evening, we transported the teens to a bowling alley and then to the YMCA to finish off the activities. Breakfast at Five Pines culminated the event at 6:00 a.m. The teens would eat outside. We borrowed a portable packing shed from one of our neighboring farms and served breakfast from it. After an all night activity the teens didn't really care how breakfast was served.

The second year we moved the dinner portion to our local middle school cafeteria with a western theme. But, the following year we had to arrange the program to be held at the Mendel Center at Lake

Michigan College as our crowds grew to over 200 young people! That year we focused on a nautical theme of *Fishers of Men,* and we served breakfast at Tiscornia Beach on the shores of Lake Michigan.

We were blessed with multi-talented people, and every year their ideas would just flow off the top of their heads. They would help us build elaborate stage settings, and we dressed as hosts to fit the theme. We were never sure if the teens or the people who hosted the event had more fun.

One young man, Dean, was an artist who drew the original artwork for the brochures, but he also served as the hilarious emcee at the banquets. His monologues had us all in stitches every year. Our prom alternative program enabled us to have an outstanding outreach to area youth, and it helped fill a need for young people in Berrien County. But after about five years the local high schools began holding their own all-night after prom activities, so we felt that there was no longer a need for this kind of program. We would focus our energies elsewhere.

᠑ ᠑ ᠑ ᠑ ᠑ ᠑ ᠑

All Night New Year's Eve Parties

With the completion of the barn project we now had an Activity Center. On New Year's Eve 1984, we hosted our first annual all-night New Year's Eve party. Eighty young people were in attendance. We felt God wanted Five Pines to be an inter-denominational ministry, and our first all-night party involved youth from many denominations. The event was continually held each New Year's Eve for over twenty years, with a high attendance of 144 teens one year. The event kept the kids off the streets and gave us an extended amount of time to have lots of group games – plus a devotional and worship. Pizza was served at midnight after a guest speaker.

Our New Year's Eve event became very popular. Weather permitting, we would let the teens tube on the tubing hill into the wee hours of the morning. The hill was lit and the run icy and fast. I clearly remember standing at the bottom of the tubing hill at 3:00 a.m. in the crisp night-time winter wonderland of God's creation. I also remember that numerous times we would take a group out skiing on the trails around 2:00 a.m. The snow would reflect the moonlight, and it was beautiful and tons of fun!

My most vivid memory was one night when we decided to take a group of teens out skiing. It was just after midnight, and the moon was bright and the snow tempting. I didn't want to teach anyone how to ski then – not at night. I asked for only those who knew how to ski, but I said yes to one I knew would be capable of picking it up real fast. I shouldn't have done that because another person (we'll call him Joe) heard me say "yes", and then he also begged to go. It was against my better judgment because I knew he lacked the coordination to meet the challenge – but I let him go. We skied on the trails not only on Five Pines property but also on the 180 acres of neighboring property that we leased for hayride and ski trails.

When we were on the *farthest part* of the trail, Joe yelled out from the top of a high hill, "Judy, I lost my glasses!"

I was at the bottom of the hill so I just said, "Put your hands down in the snow and see if you can find them," He replied, "I don't know where I lost them. I put them in my pocket when we left the barn."

That was probably an hour ago. I knew from his skiing ability that he had fallen numerous times, and only God knew where he might have lost his glasses. I couldn't do anything in the dark of the night, so I said we'll have to wait until morning. He was not happy with waiting because he said his mother would be very upset. He wanted to find his glasses *now*. Well that wasn't going to work out, not at 3:00 in the morning in the dark. The next day I skied the trails and sure enough, thirteen "craters" in the snow later, I found his glasses.

Our all night New Years Eve parties continued for many years. Here is a favorite story from our staff:

The date was December 31, 1994, and we had forty

door prizes to give away. Every teen had a number, and our staff person, Mike, was drawing numbers throughout the night (and morning!). Another staff person noticed a girl who had been alone and appeared depressed most of the night. She seemed frustrated every time a number was announced – and she didn't win. That staff person noticed her number was 70, and he walked over to Mike and said, "Whatever number you draw next, say number 70 is our next winner! Make it a good prize, too." His hand was already pulling the number out. He pulled out the slip of paper, unfolded it, and what was the number? 70! This girl excitedly claimed as her prize a nice Christian T-shirt. She couldn't believe her eyes – and neither could we. It sure is fun to watch God work.

ЯЯЯЯЯЯЯ

TWA – Teens With Alternatives

Five Pines had now increased the opportunities to reach into the lives of teens. The completion of the Harv Chrouser Activity Center enabled us to really expand our programming. In 1984 we had a group of teens who really wanted to get their unsaved friends out to Five Pines. They also expressed a desire to start an organization against drugs and alcohol. They knew friends who were involved in drugs, and the teens wanted to help them stop. They also wanted Five Pines to provide more alternative activities like the alcohol-free New Year's Eve party.

So we began Teens With Alternatives (TWA). Our dedicated teens began to hold car washes, bake sales, and different activities to raise money to begin drug-free programs. The first summer of TWA, we took a van full of teens to a drug-free conference in Atlanta. This conference opened their eyes to the goals they had for their program.

Eventually they raised enough money to purchase a complete

set of large, professional-type hand puppets along with the tapes with programming against drugs, alcohol, and smoking. Jim and I made a large portable puppet stage out of PVC pipe. We could easily break down the stage and transport it to and from performances.

The puppet show turned out to be an outstanding success. Each presentation would consist of one show on drugs, one on smoking, and one on drinking. The puppets were similar to ones you might see on television, and two of them also had sleeves to insert the puppeteer's arms. The teens did an outstanding job, and the taped programs were both funny and very informative. The students we presented the programs to loved it and so did the administrators of the schools.

In fact, one year the police chief from a local town gave TWA $500 to do all the elementary schools in his system. All in all we had about thirty teens involved in this program and ran it very successfully for about five years. The puppets and dedicated teens opened the door to share the ministry of Five Pines and relate what Five Pines was all about.

Over the period of years that we offered the TWA program, we met many, many teens who had been through drug rehab. Not all the stories were good. We knew teens who were convicted of drug charges when they only sold caffeine tablets in school. They were sent to rehab, where they were more or less forced to confess their involvement in all the drugs they were taking – and then come clean in a peer pressure setting.

Some of these kids were sent to rehab by worried parents and came out using harder drugs than when they went in. Many did not take hard drugs but confessed to all kinds of drugs so that their confessions seemed as impressive as the others. It was a sad situation, but the Lord did some mighty things in the lives of the teens that were faithfully involved in TWA. They started coming to other programs at Five Pines, heard about the Lord, and got saved.

A young man named David came to TWA. He had been in drug rehab for a number of months. David was really a very nice young man, but his life was not easy. His mother was dying from cancer, and there was very little money in the family. His mother did everything possible to see that David was at Five Pines. She was deeply concerned about him.

One day, Jim led David to the Lord as they sat in Jim's office. David slowly changed his life and the Lord was working in his heart. Just when we thought his life was getting straightened around, David was killed in an automobile crash. We were grateful that there weren't any drugs involved in the accident. David had kept his commitment and stayed drug free. But we were even more grateful that Jim was faithful and shared the Lord with him. We have always believed that David sincerely repented, saw his need for a Savior, and someday we will rejoice with him in heaven. It is so easy to put off sharing our faith with others, but Jim took the opportunity God gave him. We had no idea that David's life would be very short.

"Why, you do not even know what will happen tomorrow. What is your life? You are a mist that appears for a little while and then vanishes." – James 4:14

"But in your hearts set apart Christ as Lord. Always be prepared to give an answer to everyone who asks you to give the reason for the hope that you have. But do this with gentleness and respect." – 1 Peter 3:15

Another young man came to Five Pines to fulfill the three hundred community service hours he had been assigned to fulfill by a judge. He had been involved in an automobile fatality accident but felt the judge was up for reelection and kind of threw the book at him.

I recall the very first time I met "Ken" and had a conversation with him. He was pulling weeds behind the Activity Center, and I sat down with him. As we pulled weeds out of the mulch under a big elm tree, we began to talk. He told me how he loved to cook dinner for his mother. He was from a single-parent home and seemed very dedicated to his mother. He would come home from school and begin to prepare the evening meal before she came home from work. I was taken back by his knowledge and ability to stir up some very impressive meals.

All the time Ken was with us, I kept wondering about the three hundred community hours he was required to fulfill (when there never was proof that the accident was his fault). Ken was with us for quite a while and we really enjoyed him, he was such a nice young men. He lived about ten miles from Five Pines and sometimes rode his bike. Occasionally we had to pick him up and take him home because he couldn't drive. (His license was taken away.) We went to his graduation open house, and then he went on to the University of Michigan. We only heard from him once after that. Ken knew the Bible and was open to our sharing Christ. He was very receptive – but only God knows his heart.

☙ ☙ ☙ ☙ ☙ ☙ ☙

Fifth Quarter Begins

It was exciting to see our youth ministry continue to grow. In 1984 our Fifth Quarter program ran from 7:00 to 11:00 p.m. Because it was on Friday nights, some teens would go to their school's basketball or football game with their friends and then come out to Five Pines afterward. At other times they just didn't go to the game and came early. Teens who came to the annual New Year's Eve event, the yearly Non-Prom, or the TWA program began to come on a regular basis to Fifth Quarter as well.

The increased attendance drew unsaved young people more and more, and they were coming to Fifth Quarter and getting saved. Five Pines was becoming the place to be on Friday nights! We had young people coming from a 20 mile radius.

In 1988 Nancy Poling became our Youth Ministry Coordinator, and our attendance increased greatly (up to seventy teens per night). Nancy related well with the teens, and Five Pines was a great place to come. They knew that they were accepted. We were dealing with teens from abusive situations, kids who had a past of drug involvement, and many who felt they didn't belong anywhere else.

Five Pines was church to some who didn't go to church, and we did encourage all of the young people to start going to church. The salvation message was shared each night, and the importance of a relationship with Christ was a common topic. Not always were these teens openly accepted in the local churches. Sometimes there were comments like, "They must be from Five Pines!"

We began doing team-building activities and built some low ropes elements. We continued throughout the summer when attendance grew, and we had tons of opportunities to build a strong ownership within the large group of teens. This ownership encouraged them to bring more friends and ministry became even more exciting. We divided the seventy-plus teens into four or five groups and did competitions throughout the summer. The groups picked names, created identities, and God brought together a "family feeling". God allowed us to offer what the teens in our area needed.

Sometimes we would do all-day activities like a crazy scavenger hunts where the teens traveled to different places to find the clues. One group climbed into canoes on Lake Chapin and canoed out to an island to find their sought-after clue. While another group traveled to a place where they found bikes to bike out to where their clue was, another rode horses to find their clue and on and on until all groups finally returned to Five Pines. In closing the event we shared a meal and with a devotion from Matthew 13:44 on values and the real treasure of knowing Jesus Christ.

We often did destination unknowns to places like a water park in Wisconsin Dells, Cedar Point Theme Park in Ohio or downtown Chicago for a visit of the museums.

On the Chicago adventure two young men had different ideas. They headed off on their own "destination unknown". They left the museum, hailed a cab, and headed for their own adventure of exploring the Sears Tower. Hours later, after much prayer and anxiety on our part, our two "explorers" showed up in their taxi. One of the participants of this big town adventure has been mentioned earlier in our memoirs as a very adventurous young man, and he never failed to amaze us in the challenges he presented. *(Remember this was way before cell phones!)*

Over the years, the Fifth Quarter program constantly re-invented itself. The Lord gave us hundreds of different activities that were unique, creating an environment that brought community to this group of teens. Weekly we shared God's Word and sometimes offered opportunities for silence and solitude.

Our young people were from such diversified backgrounds, but there was a common ground of need. Every devotional found its way to speak to each person about: life, relationships, parents, sin, life and death, and about a personal relationship with Jesus Christ. Much of this teaching was new to many of these young hearts, and many came to a new-found relationship with Jesus Christ.

Over a period of time, we seemed to have one person or another living with us. These young people needed a place to think things through after an incident at home, and we would take them in. We would *always* clear this "move in with Jim and Judy" with the parents. We learned early that stories from teens did not always match up with the stories from parents. But we needed to help get things right and we used God's Word as the basis for everything in life. The basic teaching from the seminars we took some years ago helped us to understand what sin and neglect of the Word could do in a life.

I recall how a few of the youth were surprised and made comments about the fact that the dining room table was set. Most of the comments were, "Wow, are we are having a fancy meal?" In reality it was just a simple meal, but we all sat down at the table and all ate together. It wasn't *"pop it into the microwave and eat alone."* Examples like this gave us insight into what was going on in many homes – not much family time together. We were family.

There was one high school student who lived with his mother, in a very small house just down the road. He slept in the living room on the sofa since he didn't have a bed. His older brothers were dealing drugs, so this living room was busy all night long. "Tim" never could get any sleep, and yet he was up every morning trying to go to school. This young man lived with us on and off for a couple of years. He knew his Bible backward and forward, and at one point he probably witnessed to more people than we ever did. He brought many of his friends to Five Pines and witnessed to them with much boldness. He was a fun-loving boy, easy to love, and was one of our best puppeteers for TWA.

He stayed straight and clean when he lived with us, but he went back to a life of drugs when he returned home. The last time he came back and needed a place to live, he was different and I was uncomfortable. He wasn't the "Tim" we knew before. It has been many years since we have seen him, and any stories we hear have not been good. We pray that "Tim" would one day come back from the destroying life he has chosen. Jesus offers us life, and He alone can forgive and save.

Another story stands out in my mind. A large young man from a nearby town frequently attended our Fifth Quarter ministry. He appeared rough and mean and had a rather bad reputation (especially at Five Pines).

His reputation went before him, and people would ask us about the tall blond at Five Pines. More than once he would tell all kinds of wild stories about how he was with a bunch of guys who were drinking, and the police were after them. He'd tell us how he spent the night in jail and that his father had to come down and get him out. We never knew what was truth and what was fabricated.

One night we just asked him outright about these stories. He broke down and admitted that most of them weren't true. He said he didn't have anything important to talk about, so he just made up stories. We were people who would listen. He also told us that the only way he could get his father's attention was to have him come down to the police station and pick him up. We found ourselves drawn to young people like this young man, and they were drawn to Five Pines.

Some years later, this young man showed up out of the blue with a very nice girl. He said they were engaged to be married and invited us to his wedding. He was so proud and said she was the best thing that had happened to him. "She keeps me clean and straight," he explained. They were attending church and getting married in a church.

About twelve years later on a very winter day, he showed up as a chaperone for his son's school outing. He was so very proud! He said, "This is my son, and he is not like me at all! Please don't tell my son all those stories about me when I came out here in high school." Jim and I knew that we were the friends he needed affirmation from, and the other kids at Fifth Quarter were the support group he needed to get him through those difficult years of high school. In all the years he was at Five Pines, he was made aware of his sin, Christ's redemption, and what a personal relationship with Christ meant. We are not sure where that seed fell and if it took.

Twenty-seven years later, God again brought him back into our lives. We had another opportunity to witness God's love to him. In fact, he has more needs now than he has ever had: health issues, divorce, and lack of a job. But he listens and is drawn to us as we are to him. He knows the message of God's love we have to offer. That is really what he wants to hear, but he rejects "the gift" (even as desperate as he is). How sad it is.

Early in the 5th Quarter ministry one of our regular teens brought a very beautiful young lady from a local high school to Five Pines. One day when we were transporting "Tammy" with some other teens in our van, Jim and I overheard her and some other girls talking. All the girls were relating what they would like to do when they got out of high school. The new young lady stated that some day she thought she would like to be a prostitute. "Tammy's" mother had told her that prostitutes had pretty clothes, and men spent a lot of money on them.

Jim and I were shocked to say the least, but we were privileged to minister to this beautiful girl all of her high school years through Five Pines Fifth Quarter. She even went with us on some wilderness trips and also worked the puppets for TWA.

Tammy was a very personable, loveable, and vivacious young lady. Occasionally she brought her younger sister to Fifth Quarter, but we found her to be very reserved and rather withdrawn. One day the mother of these two girls called in tears. She said that the child protective services were at her house to take her children from her. We went over immediately. Her husband, step-father to the girls, had been accused of sexually abusing the girls. The mother adamantly denied that her husband was guilty, but later we found out that he was very much guilty. He was eventually sent to prison for a very long term.

We lost track of Tammy after she graduated from high school. Later we heard she had moved out of state and was dancing in a nightclub. A few years later, we heard she was married and had a wonderful husband and a number of children. Then one day a staff person found her on Facebook. Tammy stated that she was happily married and what she loved most were: reading her Bible, praying, and teaching her children about Christ's imminent return to take His own. Yes, there was a victory in Christ. She said, "I am one of His!" Amen.

Jim and I had to be incredibly consistent in teaching from God's Word. Most of the time it was a new way of understanding their relationships with their parents, their siblings, and also how they saw themselves. God's Word was the solid ground to base these life applications on. It would help them see their sin as God saw it, help them stand up to the pressures of their peers, lead them to Christ-like life, and direct them into a purpose-driven life.

We directed the Fifth Quarter program every Friday night for the first ten years. It was a most rewarding part of our involvement in a ministry we never dreamed of. God supplied us with an outstanding program, faithful volunteers, strong parent support, and a ton of eager young people.

I believe we will never know the numbers of decisions for Christ through this program, but the revival God did in those early years of Fifth Quarter was sensational. Thirty years later people tell us how those years at Five Pines impacted their lives. We even have a number of couples who met at Five Pines, got married, and now send their children to Five Pines programs. Exactly what Harv Chrouser told us would happen. A seed is planted; it grows, and produces fruit.

ꊣ ꊣ ꊣ ꊣ ꊣ ꊣ ꊣ

Five Pines Live

When Jim Wing joined our staff in 1991, he moved the Fifth Quarter program to a new high. He changed the event to Saturday nights and called it Five Pines Live (FPL). Jim brought our youth ministry to a deeper spiritual level and faithfully sacrificed every Saturday night ministering to hundreds of teens for the next ten years. I once read a statement someone wrote about FPL:

- *Imagine a youth ministry that is the teen's number one priority on a Saturday night.*
- *Imagine a youth ministry where the participants ask for longer times of praise!*
- *Imagine a youth ministry where the teens ask for an all worship night.*
- *Imagine a youth ministry where teens are free to share their deepest concerns, without the threat of being humiliated.*
- *You don't have to imagine! It's real – "Five Pines Live". This dynamic ministry of outreach and caring and worship is the experience every Saturday evening by an average of forty-five young people.*

One year near the Easter season, a large rugged-looking cross appeared on the front of the stage area. Jim explained to the fifty-four teens what the Bible said about Jesus' death on the cross. "Jesus suffered a cruel and humiliating death publicly for you and me," he continued. "It's not too much to ask for you to stand publicly among your peers if you would like to accept Jesus as your Lord and Savior."

As they waited and quietly prayed, three girls in the back stood up one at a time, and there was rejoicing in heaven! Everyone celebrated these teens taking a stand for Jesus Christ. Three female staff met with the girls to talk and pray. Two were for salvation and one was a recommitment.

Following the invitation, each person wrote the sins they struggled with on a piece of paper and came forward to "nail" those sins to the cross. It was a "no-condemnation" reminder (Romans 8:1) as well as a challenge to "lay aside the sin that so easily entangles us"

(Hebrews 12:1).

One year the teens chose the theme "Awestruck"; celebrating God in awe of who He is. How these young people had grown! It was amazing at what was happening in their lives. Periodically we would receive letters that expressed exciting statements of God's activity in their lives. One letter read:

"I love Five Pines Live because I feel 'spurred on' and encouraged (Hebrews 10:23-25) after each meeting. It is inspiring to spend time with people my own age who have a passion for God. The things that go on inside that big red barn on Saturday nights have positively impacted my life and my future."

Our prayer was that what went on in "that big red barn" on Saturday nights would glorify God and direct teens to obey Him through His Word. Jim Wing shared the highlights of his years with the FPL group:

- Twenty to thirty minutes of spontaneous, Spirit-led worship with teens.
- One Saturday night at 11:45, a 17-year-old boy said to me, "I'd like to be saved, but I don't know what to do." At 12:30 a.m., a simple prayer of faith was uttered and heaven rejoiced.
- Sometimes God *totally* changed the plan we had for the night. It always worked because His Spirit was leading, and the staff would follow in anticipation of great thing happening.
- One girl showed up for the first time, and I knew her from a nearby ministry. After our worship time, she asked me, "Is it always like this?" I smiled and said, "Pretty much."
- When Jim Wing left in 2005, our office manager Mike Emerson took over the FPL program. Mike actually met his wife, Karen, at Fifth Quarter.

In 2006, a group of twenty-nine teens and adults from FPL spent a week helping rebuild homes as Hurricane Katrina relief in Louisiana. This fabulous group of young people also raised money for the International Justice Mission, an evangelical Christian organization whose mission is to combat citizen's rights abuse (including sex trafficking, sexual violence, and slavery). They also supported a

Compassion Child for a number of years, and when one of the volunteers faced a critical health problem, the FPL bunch raised $1,000 to help her with medical expenses. Young people demonstrated they have heart and want a purpose in life.

One student thanked us for helping her walk through her four years of high school, helping her stay faithful to the Lord, and always feeling she had a special place to go – a place where people cared and loved her and supported her in times of need. Another young man said, "Five Pines Live is someplace I can go on Saturday nights where Satan doesn't tempt me." It meant he didn't have to be alone; where he could meet and have Christian friends from around the county.

I think this letter sums up what Five Pines Live was like more than any other letter.

Dear Friends,

Why do I like Five Pines Live? Why do I make my parents drag me out to Berrien Center every week and make my dad come back out later than he should be on Saturday nights?

I think the first thing that struck me about Five Pines Live was the fact that everyone there wants to be there. I've noticed too often that kids are at church youth groups because their parents make them go, not because they enjoy it.

Another thing is that Five Pines Live is kind of like the church. Christ is the head, he's behind the wheel, he's the coach in the huddle. However you want to think about it, everything rests on him. But the people are the ones making up the team. We all support and encourage each other, and there is no feeling of being left out or left behind. Nobody is left on the bench.

My favorite part of the night is worship. The focus isn't on the musicians or people standing next to you. It's all about worshiping God. It's all about slowing down for just once in our busy lives and telling God just how great He is and how thankful we are.

So why do I like Five Pines Live? Sure, I've made friends there. I know kids from all over southwestern Michigan. And, yeah, I love the encouragement that I get. But the best part is that everyone's main purpose is to find God, love Him, and spread that love around to everyone else. If you come, you will probably know what I'm talking about. If you can't get a ride, walk! Yeah, it's that impressive.

We never expected rewards in this life, but these small hand-written notes spoke for hundreds of teens who found solace during their difficult years in high school at a small ministry called Five Pines. God had worked in this ministry and provided a place for these young people to go, a group they belonged to, and a message that many a young heart wanted to hear. Jesus loves you, and He has a plan for your lives! To some of our participants, Five Pines was church to them; a place they learned about Christ as their Lord and Savior and the value of God's Word as a direction for their lives. *Grandpa Albert would be happy!*

The influence of these programs was far beyond our perspective. We've witnessed the message, the seed, and the mysterious power it has to change lives. We have witnessed young people grow in their relationship with Christ and are now pastors, missionaries, and parents of children involved at Five Pines. We read of Christ's love in 2 Corinthians 5:14-15. His love has a compelling virtue to excite ministries and entice simple people like Jim and Judy, Jim Wing, Terry Mason, and Mike and Karen Emerson (and many others) to challenge young people to a relationship with Christ and a purpose for life in serving the "Great I Am" (John 8:58).

EIGHTEEN

Full Time – A Big Step of Faith

"Trust in the Lord with all your heart and lean not on your own understanding; in all your ways acknowledge him, and he will make your paths straight." –
Proverbs 3:5-6

AS TIME WENT ON, it was just becoming too difficult for either of us to do Five Pines part time and still work at our outside jobs. Jim took the huge step first and then I followed.

Jim left his job at Whirlpool Corporation in 1984 to work as the full-time director of Five Pines. I held onto my part-time job at Southwestern Medical Clinic for three more years. Even though I was only part time, I felt secure with the little money I made. At least it could buy groceries! Don Gast, the director of SWMC, wanted me to stay on for the total eleven years to guarantee a pension. We always appreciated how Don looked after us. His loving insight protected us from making rash decisions.

The ministry itself did not have enough income to support us, and we never expected to take any income directly from the ministry. Our board of directors suggested that we go on a missionary support system. This meant we would endeavor to raise support from individuals for our income and totally trust the Lord.

I was the non-trusting one. Time and time again I would say, "Jim, show me where the money is going to come from and then you can go full time."

Jim finally said, "Judy, you are not trusting God. He will supply when we let go and trust Him – and not until."

God provided us with generous supporters who loved the Lord and trusted us. They trusted that we also loved the Lord and would serve Him in whatever way He led us and the ministry. I love the verse from the hymn, *"Trust and obey for there's no other way to be happy in Jesus, but to trust and obey."* We stepped out and trusted in the beginning and have ever since.

"Those who trust in themselves are fools, but those who walk in wisdom are kept safe." – Proverbs 28:26

We had no choice but to trust the Lord. God blessed us with a group of supporters who have been ever so faithful. Many have continued their support for over thirty years. That has been a phenomenal dedication to the Lord and His work here at Five Pines. We have been privileged to take an unbelievable walk with the Lord and with the support of people who love Him.

ဆ ဆ ဆ ဆ ဆ ဆ ဆ

The Fabric of Friendship

"So Joshua fought the Amalekites as Moses had ordered, and Moses, Aaron and Hur went to the top of the hill. As long as Moses held up his hands, the Israelites were winning, but whenever he lowered his hands, the Amalekites were winning. When Moses' hands grew tired, they took a stone and put it under him and he sat on it. Aaron and Hur held his hands up—one on one side, one on the other—so that his hands remained steady till sunset. So Joshua overcame the Amalekite army with the sword." – Exodus 17:10-13

This story of Joshua's battle with the Amalekites has so many similarities to where we were in our walk with the Lord:

1. Joshua was early in his training to take over the leadership from Moses to lead God's people into the Promised Land. This was his very first battle of many to come. Jim had just left his job at Whirlpool and stepped into the director's shoes of a new youth ministry.

2. The soldiers under Joshua's leadership were undisciplined and ill-equipped – weak in every way. Jim and I were both "green" by all standards in directing this new adventure of following the Lord.

3. Moses was visible to the army holding up the staff to demonstrate his support of the troops. Holding up his hands was an intercession appeal to God, pleading for success and victory. Jim and his board of directors had been faithful to bring every step of the early developments of the ministry before the Lord.

4. Aaron and Hur were important in their support of Moses. Holding up the arms of a weary Moses was critical to his intercession and their victory. In the beginning of Five Pines, we witnessed the timely Hand of God providing the precious and faithful Aarons and Hurs in our ministry.

God led us into a prayer group of believers who met on Monday nights. Pastor Den Slattery and his wife, Karen, opened their home and their hearts to us and about six other couples. The men met in the living room to pray, and all women went into Den's office. Week after week our group of women sat on the floor of his office praying. Sometimes there were many tears, crying out to God for forgiveness, healing, or understanding. Week after week we literally agonized in prayer for over an hour on the needs and challenges God had set before us.

Our group had many special issues only known to God that came up during those seven years together. We faithfully prayed for:

- one of our couple's two-year-old son who had just been diagnosed with leukemia
- a couple's teenage daughter who was pregnant
- a farmer about to lose his farm
- a daughter about to be married in rebellion to the parent's wishes
- a man working on his doctorate and his need for finances as his wife homeschooled their three children
- Jim and Judy desiring to know God's will for their lives and the ministry of Five Pines (including hiring another full-time staff person).

Over the years this prayer group grew so very close. Couples moved away and new couples joined us. These dear people became our closest friends and our most faithful group of supporters. We all shared our hearts and our tears and our prayers with each other. This tightly-knit group was a most beautiful gift of God. He knew we would need this kind of a support group, and in turn it was a blessing to be supportive of others. They were people who cared, who believed, and who loved the Lord from the depths of their hearts.

Jim and I both feel they were the Aarons and Hurs of our lives, people who were there to help us lift our hearts to the Lord and pray for His guidance. We cherish those precious times. How often we refer back to those prayer meetings; those great nights of such loving fellowship and the strength we all absorbed from each other. God continued to weave all these people into the beautiful Tapestry of His ministry at Five Pines. They were supporting threads that helped make a firm tapestry.

য় য় য় য় য় য় য়

Christian Camping & Conference Association – CCCA

"From Him the whole body, joined and held together by every supporting ligament, grows and builds itself up in love, as each part does its work." – Ephesians 4:16

In the beginning when we worked with just a few young people, we sought help with programming and attended a youth ministry workshop at Moody Bible College. It wasn't long before we decided we didn't really seem to fit there. At the workshop, people asked us questions like: "What church are you youth pastors at?" "What is your role?" "How big is your youth group?" Our answer was usually, "Well, we really aren't a church youth group, but we ..."

Harv Chrouser had encouraged us to get involved in our state's CCCA organization, an international Christian Camping and Conference Association. I was overwhelmed the first time we attended the three-day meeting of the Michigan Sectional. Here were all these camp directors and staff from many great Christian camps all over the state of Michigan. They were contemplating how they would fill their three hundred or five hundred beds for their summer camp programs. Many were program directors or wilderness program directors.

When we sat down at our meals, people were very friendly and would introduce themselves. Then they asked: "Where is your camp?" "What do you do at camp?" "How many beds do you have?" I would just shrink down in my seat. We didn't have *any* beds or *any* buildings, nor did we have a staff. We didn't have a degree in wilderness programming either.

Introducing ourselves was very uncomfortable – especially for me. We were just two simple people who wanted to serve God and felt a calling to work with youth. We were just plain people with an old barn, an overgrown farm, and a burning heart to serve the Lord.

We didn't seem to fit in with anyone! People weren't rude; we just didn't seem to belong. But soon we felt the warmth of these very special people. Degrees in something great didn't matter with these people. They accepted our desires and welcomed us into their specialty: "Sharing God's wonderful outdoors and His love with children at camp." We soon learned that CCCA consisted of wonderful veteran camp directors who lovingly came alongside us and encouraged Jim in all his programming and building ventures. Harv was right!

Enoch Olsen, founder of Spring Hill Camps, a giant in the world of Christian camping, spent a weekend with us and was a tremendous encouragement. Jean and Kermit Hanley, of Eagle Village, took us under their expertise and demonstrated a real interest into the venture we felt God was leading us to. Bob Tissot, director of Bair Lake Camp, and Steve and Kathy Prudhomme, directors from Grace Adventures, shared their hearts with us on many occasions.

They were leaders in CCCA nationwide (even worldwide), but they cared about the little Five Pines camp and Jim and Judy. CCCA's annual Michigan sectional meeting held in the spring enriched our lives with tremendous speakers and workshops. We learned much of the basis of our programs and philosophy at CCCA.

Harv Chrouser continued in prayer and communication with us in such a caring way until the Lord called him home. We were not too small for any of these giants of the Christian camping ministries. These were people who have supported camping ministries around the world. They helped Christian camps begin in Russia in locations that one day was used to indoctrinate children in communism. They helped camps get started in Brazil, other South American countries, and China. Great people who were known worldwide, and yet they gave us unlimited time and advice. They had a boldness that came from the love of their hearts for the Lord and their belief that God uses large and small Christian camps – and Jim and Judy.

NINETEEN

Appalachian Weavings – Smoky Mountain Trips

"It is God who arms me with strength and makes my way perfect. He makes my feet like the feet of a deer; he enables me to stand on heights." – Psalm 18:32-33

A YEAR OR SO after we began attending Berrien Center Bible Church, the leadership asked us to be one of the sponsors for the church's junior high youth group. We would work with Dean and Jean Whitney and Pastor Schoen and his wife, Joan. One of the activities was a summer camping trip to the Smoky Mountains in Gatlinburg, Tennessee. In the summer of 1981, we were introduced to what is one of the most beautiful parts of our wonderful country. We immediately fell in love with the Smoky Mountains, the people, and the contrasting way of life they offered.

On one hand, there were the hundreds of hiking trails into the mountains and the challenge each offered; the unique Appalachian Trail, its history, and the beauty of a vast array of creeks and cascading waterfalls throughout the mountains. There was also the rich culture of the hill country people. The history of their pioneers and the simplicity of their lifestyles drew our interest.

We did fall in love with all that this area offered us, not only in our private lives but also as a source of challenge to young people involved in Five Pines programming. It was only a twelve-hour trip traveling by van from Berrien Center, Michigan, to the Smokies. That location turned out to be very affordable as well as within a day's driving distance.

In 1986, Jim decided to start the tradition of a spring break backpacking trip in the Smoky Mountains. The snow would be gone or almost gone in the mountains. Students would be looking for something to do, and the trip would meet our ministry purpose statement of challenging both physically and spiritually.

When we planned our first trip, one of the eight participants who signed up for the first trip was Wendy a participant in Fifth Quarter. Her parents annually spent the spring break week down in Gatlinburg, Tennessee, and were willing to spot the van for the group from the trailhead to the pick-up point. I spent the week previous to the trip packing all the food. I followed Dr. Roach's method of packing food for the Boundary Water trips and then spent the week of the trip at home in much prayer!

The first trip was a great success, encouraging, and uneventful. Jim was excited and so were the teens that went. We felt that annual spring break trips to the Smokies and Boundary Water canoe trips in late summer would be the focus of Five Pines' wilderness challenge programs. God wanted us to add to our tapestry the rugged wilderness experiences His phenomenal creation offered.

ଛ ଛ ଛ ଛ ଛ ଛ ଛ

A City Girl Needs to Get Rugged!

"But he said to me, 'My grace is sufficient for you, for my power is made perfect in weakness.'" – 2 Corinthians 12:9

The next year as we organized the Smokies trip, a question came up about who the female staff person would be. We had a girl participant who was a senior in high school, but we needed a female adult.

It was Easter Sunday and the backpacking trip was to leave the next day. Oops. We *still* didn't have an adult female staff going, and Jim looked at me! Well, Jim had been working with the participants by hiking in their new boots (feet are important on a trip like this) and walking up and down the tubing hill with their backpacks on. The packs were filled with heavy books to get the feeling of the additional *fifty pounds* they would carry on their backs. Now *one day* before the trip,

Jim looked at me and said, "You are going to have to go!"

My response to Jim: "Oh, waitaminute! I don't have hiking boots nor have I *ever* had a backpack on, and I am not in shape to attack the mountains!" At church that morning hiking boots in my size (that were already broken in) were offered to me. A backpack "just my size" was also provided. God often works in ways like that! On Monday I found myself in the van headed for a week of hiking in the Smokies with six students and Jim.

The trailhead Jim chose began at Clingman's Dome, the highest point in the Smokies. We would be hiking down the mountain most of the first part of the trip. Our trail followed a dried up drainage bed for the first three hours of hiking. We were going down, down, down, all the way. When someone is hiking in the mountains, they use certain muscles to climb up and different muscles going down steep trails (and a different kind of pain in your legs). I had a backpack on my back for the first time ever, climbing over huge fallen trees and attempting to get my footing on shale rock.

I constantly felt like I would fall, land on my back, and not being able to get up (much like a turtle on his back). The students were patient with me, my rugged walking stick proved a lifesaver, and we finally got to our first campsite. I could take that pack off my back!

As we began to set up camp and begin dinner, one of our participants complained of a stomach ache. As the darkness set in and only our small campfire providing light, our hiker curled up in his tent and began to cry out as his pain increased. Jim and I feared it was appendicitis.

As the nighttime blackness crept into our remote campsite, we began to feel more and more cut off from civilization and alone in the wilderness on the mountain. We were five miles in from the trailhead at the uppermost point in the mountains and an almost impossible trail to backtrack on. (Granted a cell phone would have been great to have, but this was before cell phones, and there probably wouldn't have been any service there.) We had no communication, no medical personnel, and the only answer was prayer.

Jim was in the tent and trying to comfort the hiker. As I joined the rest of the group huddled together, we looked up at the star-filled night and pleaded in prayer that God would intercede and heal our friend.

The night seemed to drag on and on, but in the morning our hiker was free of pain. God had protected us and afforded our small group a tremendous lesson of His faithfulness. 1 Corinthians 2:9 came to mind: *"No eye has seen, no ear has heard, no mind has conceived what God has prepared for those who love Him."*

We had no idea what challenges God had for us. This first Smoky Mountain trip for me was only the beginning of many eye-opening experiences in which God would reveal Himself to us. We stepped out in faith, God had promised to never leave us or forsake us, and He alone would fill our lives with an awesome walk with Him.

I had a tendency to slow up the pace of hiking because I was not in shape and somewhat older than the young teens. To counteract my slow pace, we had one eager young man who wanted to move at a pace one step short of running. He consistently got out of sight and ended up at our next campsite sometimes *hours* before we got there. Time and time again we said, "Mike, you must stay with the group!" We feared that he would miss the trail and take off on another trail – thereby being lost in a very large area. These mountains contained *hundreds* of trails which could lead him to who knows where. But his enthusiasm took over every day as he led the way. God certainly watched over us.

One day we were on high ground, one switchback after another, climbing and climbing. I learned to not look up because I would get discouraged. Would we ever get to the top? My legs became moving objects with no feeling. They just went forward, one step at a time, on and on for what seemed like *forever*. My legs finally got me to the next campsite. This hiking in the mountains was by no means easy, but I loved it.

The next day we were on lower ground among the rhododendron, redbuds, and dogwood, and our hiking trail led us to five or six creek crossings. The low ground offered us the beauty of moss growing on logs and ferns and trillium all over the valley. We often hiked anywhere from eight to ten miles a day. I began to like this new venture God had led us into, and Jim and I grew more in love with the Smokies.

As I eagerly readied myself for my second Smokies trip in 1988, a friend at church asked me if there was anything she could do while we were gone. I said, "Just pray because I know from past experiences that God always seems to allow new challenges on any wilderness trip." Dr. Roach had taught us that God always provides the teaching tools for these wilderness trips as well. I hiked up and down the tubing hill everyday for a full month with a backpack full of encyclopedias on my back.

I couldn't wait to enjoy God's beautiful creation again. I so enjoyed the challenge of the trip: the warmth of the sun as we hiked, the quietness of the mountains, and the tiny little streams cascading down the mountains. I felt like we were alone with God, and we were. It was an exhilarating feeling. I was hooked. Having been raised in the city, these outdoor experiences were new and challenging. I stepped out of the boat again and had to trust God.

Our trailhead began this time in lower ground on the southern part of the mountains, and we started our trek by going through a tunnel. It was a hot day and all of us on the trip had shorts on. It was early April so there weren't any leaves on the trees yet, and the sun was beating directly down on us. At one point we stopped at a small creek and put wet bandanas around our necks.

That night as the sun slowly set and we made dinner, it got much colder. In the middle of the night I woke up with an excruciating headache. I got out of our tent to get some aspirin from my backpack and noticed *snow* on the ground. I wanted to go back and stay in the tunnel, and Jim just laughed: "That would be a bad idea."

The next day we had a ten-hour hike up and over a major ridge. There were those horrible switchbacks again: climbing, climbing, and more climbing. Each time I looked up and took another turn on a switchback, my mind said, *"We will never get to the top."* As we got closer to noon and lunch and the top of the ridge, the weather turned much colder. We didn't pack any gloves, so we had to use our extra pair of socks on our hands to protect them from the elements. At the very top of the ridge we stopped for lunch: cheese, crackers, summer sausage, and Snickers candy bars. My fingers were too cold to even eat my lunch. I felt I would never get warm again, but we had a beautiful sight of the mountains below to warm our souls.

The trip down was somewhat easier, but a new kind of pain felt like a spike in my legs. My walking stick was my savior, but getting down to our lowland campsite was exhilarating to say the least. We started a toasty campfire, and dinner of spaghetti and applesauce and hot chocolate warmed our bodies.

In the morning when we got up to eat our warm oatmeal, we found that the water in our canteens was frozen solid. But the sun was out and we felt warm. Today we were supposed to have about six or seven creek crossings, and we were grateful for a warmer day to be challenged by the cold mountain streams. We would take off our hiking boots, put on our tennis shoes, and wade across at each creek crossing. On the other side we took off the wet tennis shoes, hung them on the back of our backpacks, and put our hiking boots back on. This kept our feet and valuable hiking boots dry.

Campsite number three offered us a beautiful stream and a great place to camp. I remember washing my hair in a bucket of water from the icy stream, and my brain felt like it was shrinking and frozen. It actually hurt my head to wash my hair, but I felt clean.

At campsite number four we were closer to our departure point and grateful to the Lord for a week of wonderful experiences. We sat around the campfire as we always did in the evenings and shared God's Word. Jim asked the hikers how they saw the Lord work that day, and it was such a blessing to hear their comments. The high school students so enjoyed being away from everything and witness the beauty of God's creation – especially the black and star-studded sky. This wilderness experience enabled us to be grateful for the little things in life: the warmth of the sun, the beauty of the mountains, and the experience of being alone with God.

One of our hikers on this trip was an exchange student from Germany, and Heidi had borrowed her hiking boots for the trip. Sometime in the evening she placed them close to the fire to dry – too close. They burned down or "melted" on the side closest to the flames. Now her boots were no longer wearable. We had only five miles to hike out the next day, and Heidi could easily just wear her tennis shoes.

But... as we woke that next morning, something was different! Laying there in our sleeping bags, we remarked that it seemed like the top of the tent was sagging. Just then we heard lots of noise coming from the boys' tents. Their tent had collapsed due to the weight of the "bushels" of *snow* that had just fallen from a pine branch hanging over their tent. A good two feet of snow fell throughout the night and now we had a challenge we didn't expect.

We were nestled in over two feet of snow and huge trees were falling all around us due to the weight of the very wet snow. Immediately our thoughts were, *"Does anyone know we are out here?"* We had trail permits and the National Park Service would know about where we were, but suddenly we felt isolated from what was going on in the world around us.

We got dressed, started a fire, heated some water for oatmeal and hot chocolate, and evaluated our circumstances. Remember that Heidi only had tennis shoes to wear. We didn't plan on snow – especially two feet of it. We decided she could wear numerous pairs of socks, put plastic bags over the socks, and find a large pair of tennis shoes from one of the guys. It worked! Her feet were probably drier and warmer than the rest of ours.

The trail was hidden at times. The thick rhododendron bushes hung heavy-laden with the weight of the snow. It was a blessing Jim had taken this trail the previous two years. One of our ambitious young men eagerly wanted to attempt to meet the challenge of breaking the trail and finding our way out. We all walked in his footsteps rather than struggle to make new footprints. Five miles and many hours later we hiked into Deep Creek Campground, and there was our van.

This may sound like a great ending to a harrowing story, but the end to our challenges didn't stop at our van. A huge tree was down across the road and we couldn't get out of the park. Our superhero teens thought they could move the tree. They could not! Then they proceeded to get out our small wood saws and attempt to cut it in half. They could not! We just needed to wait until someone came and removed the tree. Eventually someone came and cut it up.

Our saga didn't even stop there. The trailer jackknifed on the steep icy hill during our attempt to get out of the park. There was only one way out of the area and that was Interstate 40. Every road was covered with snow, and plows were unseen (at least where we were).

Finally we got on I-40 only to find semi trucks all over the side of the road and all exits blocked. All motels were full. We now began to realize that we were in one of the worst snowstorms ever to hit the Smoky Mountain area. (Remember the lady who asked what she could do while we were gone?!) We finally were able to get to a convenience store, go to the restroom, and buy what chips and soda we could. We had not really taken any showers for a week and were confined together all day in the van; obviously the odor was not very pleasant. We prayed for safety, a motel, and a shower.

After about six hours in the van, we came back around the mountains to Pigeon Forge, Tennessee, and eagerly took the first motel we could find and a good meal at the nearest restaurant. The challenges God walked us through that week will never, never be forgotten. Was it worth it? I was eager to return the next year – Praise God!

TWENTY

A Colorful Tapestry Pattern of Miracles
Summer Day Camp Begins

*"Even when I am old and gray, do not forsake me, O God, till I declare your power
to the next generation, your might to all who come."* – Psalm 71:18

HARV CHROUSER'S SUGGESTION in 1982 to start a day camp for younger children didn't seem to fit in the scope of what we thought our capabilities were. When we first became Christians, we worked with the junior high youth at our church followed by many years with the high school students in TWA and Fifth Quarter programs. Having all this experience with teenagers, we were hesitant to attempt to do programming with younger children.

But Harv continued to encourage us.

It would have to be a *miracle* – a change of heart – and a total acceptance that God alone would make this happen. Harv repeatedly told us that summer camp would be a "seed program" for all the other programs we were doing. The younger campers would grow up and be part of all the other ministry events (the Fifth Quarter/Five Pines Live program, the wilderness trips, and be counselors and staff for the day camp program). Harv was so adamant about this, but we just couldn't imagine how it would work. We had only the Activity Center and a small pool. Harv said we had a *perfect* place to start.

For three years Harv challenged us with the same question: "Did you start that day camp yet?"

For three years our answer was always the same: "We don't think we can do it."

Then a miracle happened. God began to change our hearts.

Our friends *were* eager to help and just *maybe* it would happen. I would have to start thinking more creatively if we did programming for small children. I prayed and God give me the mind of a child! You might not think that this was a miracle, but I like the thinking of Albert Einstein:

"There are only two ways to live your life. One is as though nothing is a miracle. The other is as though everything is a miracle."

So in 1985 we sent out a flyer for a Kid's Day for third and fourth grade students. We picked three dates: one day in June, one in July, and one in August. Wow! We were being so bold; three whole days of programming!

Two of our friends, Jim Markle and Rick Fedoruk, came up with a creative schedule of events and ideas. We used our small private 20-foot by 40-foot pool for swimming sessions taught by Jane Markle (Jim's wife). I did a craft in the ski room of the Activity Center, and we had games and a Bible lesson.

We did the first Kid's Day in June and it went well. Parents and campers wanted more and looked forward to the other two days in July and August. The following year we stepped out in faith and scheduled one full week of camp with a western theme.

Our goal was twenty-five campers, and the Lord blessed our efforts as we filled up our first week. Rick had some great ideas: a rodeo with a barrel race on bikes, calf-roping with a chair and lasso, and a hayride.

Jim Markle had past experience with camp programming, so he helped set up a very simple schedule of activities for the entire week. It was basically what Harv had told us to do: a Bible lesson, a nature lesson, a swim class, and crafts in the morning with games in the afternoon. We would stir up the jug of "Bug Juice" for lunch, and the campers would bring their own food. The week was a great success and gave us a glimpse of what could be.

One year later I resigned my position at Southwestern Medical Clinic to become full-time Day Camp Director. This was another giant leap of faith for Jim and me.

ဆ ဆ ဆ ဆ ဆ ဆ ဆ

An Exciting Environment of Diverse Programming

God had provided Five Pines with thirty-three acres of rural land, and Harv said, "Use it all. Let the campers explore and they will have a ball!" He believed in doing as much programming as possible in God's creation. What better way to teach them about our Great Creator! We believe that there is a profound and lasting growth when a child encounters the power and wonder of God's creation.

When we started planning our summer camp program, we sought to instill the value of the Word of God in the lives of our campers. The Bible being the unifying theme of Five Pines programming, the basis of our teaching and the life-changing truths it imparts. We would then link it to a theme that would create an exciting atmosphere for our campers. As an example our Knights in Shining Armor theme was created in the Biblical teaching of God's armor. Repetition of the theme was important. We also wanted to bring our campers into an exciting environment. We set out to accomplish this through Bible teaching, memorization of Scripture, both verbal and with sign language. The sign language brought a new depth to God's Word and a marvelous learning tool for our young campers.

1. Every camper would be challenged to understand their sinful nature and their need for forgiveness of sin through a personal relationship with Jesus Christ.
2. There would be a purpose and value to every program and activity we developed; not just fill the time.
3. Camp would be for building relationships and having fun – counselors and campers alike.
4. We would value the imaginations of our young campers and we would incorporate programs that would focus on using that imagination. We agreed with Albert Einstein theory: *"Imagination is more important than knowledge."*)

5. Each child would be challenged to learn far beyond their own expectations.

We had great expectations, and our campers and God made it possible to fulfill those expectations.

God demonstrated His faithfulness to us as we watched Him do mighty things. We wrote our purpose statement and the philosophy of what Five Pines camp would provide. Over the years many of our programs have been updated and revised, but the original purpose and philosophy of Five Pines Day Camp remains the same: "Excellence with a Purpose".

෨ ෨ ෨ ෨ ෨ ෨ ෨

Five Pines Day Camp Purpose Statement

It is our purpose to:
A. Provide a camping environment which challenges young people spiritually to a relationship with Jesus Christ and with growth and commitment to God's will for their lives.
B. Provide a camping environment that will offer each child a new and exciting experience that can broaden his/her perspective in a positive way.
C. Provide a camping experience which challenges young people in a safe environment both for their physical well-being and their emotional well-being.

Our goals, purpose, and planning were all very important. We realized, though, that it is not the experience we create, but it is God through Christ who transforms lives.

We challenged our staff to focus on activities, programming, relationships and the outdoor environment to accomplish Five Pines' objective of growing a camper in his relationship with Christ. We challenged our staff to create new and exciting camping experiences that can be built on year after year. We valued programming that instills self-confidence and discovery.

It wasn't long before we realized the importance of a simple program of bringing kids to camp and how God could use it in their lives. Five Pines summer camp could have never offered all the amenities that some larger heavily-financed camps could offer, but we could guarantee that each and every child would have a great time, be filled with excitement, be introduced to our Savior, and come home a happier kid.

"I will praise you, O Lord, with all my heart;
I will tell of all your wonders.
I will be glad and rejoice in you;
I will sing praise to your name, O Most High" – Psalm 9:1-2

☙ ☙ ☙ ☙ ☙ ☙ ☙

State Licensing

Sometime during the 1990's, in our attempt to get our day camp licensed, we found that there was only a license available for residence camps in the state of Michigan. Kathy Prudhomme was the Christian Camping liaison with the state on policies and licensing. She was a strong advocate for separate licensing for day camps and presented Five Pines programming and camper/counselor agendas to the state as a sample!

If the State would decide to license day camps, Five Pines was to be the sample for the requirements of day camp licensing. The state was impressed with our thorough presentation of our day camp procedures, and we were given the title of a premier day camp model for the state of Michigan! After many deliberations, the state decided to just require all camps to abide by the same rules for licensing; resident camps and day camps alike.

This was not a huge requirement for Five Pines, since we had been applying all resident camp licensing requirements for years even though we were only a day camp.

EVERGLADES TRIP 1980

Judy Scofield

TRANSFORMATION BARN TO

ACTIVITY CENTER 1983

ACTIVITY CENTER ADDITIONS

BOUNDARY WATERS

GOLDEN THREADS OF THE
MINISTRY

Harv Chrouser

Don Gast

1929 - 2015

Judy Scofield

EARLY   HAY RIDES

TEENS WITH ALTURNATIVES

Remodeled 1850 Home
of the Scofield's

Judy Scofield

NON-PROM 1984

APPALACHIAN WEAVINGS 1987

FIFTH QUARTER/ FIVE PINES LIVE

FIRST WEEK OF DAY CAMP

1986 & INNER CITY CAMP

SUMMER DAY CAMPS

CAMP EXPRESSIONS

MAX CHALLENGE

HIGH ROPES

Judy Scofield

STAFF FROM THE PAST

DAY CAMP CRAFTS

COUNSELORS

OUR MANY FACES OF FIVE PINES

TWENTY-ONE

Early Steps – Beginning of Day Camp

A miracle is when God breaks His usual pattern and does something extraordinary!

THE STORIES OF HOW our summer camp programming came together never cease to amaze me. Our unbelief caused us to think that this was an impossible venture. In the ninth chapter of Mark, Jesus is approached by the father of a small boy who was possessed with an evil spirit. He asked Jesus if he can do anything, take pity on them and help them. Jesus replied with a question: *"If you can?"* Then he said, *"Everything is possible for him who believes."*

God has demonstrated that what seemed impossible to us *was* possible if we just believed in Him. I love the statement: *"If you can explain what is going on, God didn't do it."*

In the beginning of our journey, we wanted to challenge the campers with a total experience from the morning when they first showed up at camp until the afternoon when they left. The theme of the summer was carried out throughout the entire week in all programming from Bible, to nature to swimming, crafts and afternoon programming.

We wanted our campers to *experience* the Bible lessons as well as all the activities incorporated into each theme. We didn't want our campers bored with the flannel graph lessons that many Sunday schools were still using. Bible lessons would be interactive with costumes and camper participation. We made robes for our young campers as they acted out the Bible stories for Psalm One of Joseph and his brothers, Samuel and Eli, and the little maiden with Naaman for our *Gold Rush Days* camp.

It was our desire to establish some very important principles concerning afternoon camper competitions. The games were chosen to be fun and help establish ownership of each camper's group. It also was important to protect each child's self-esteem, so we did not implement games whereby someone is openly a loser or where children are made fun of and laughed at.

Our camp would award *huge* amounts of points to every team. Giving large numbers of points doesn't cost anything and encourages the last-place team to cheer as well because they had *17,000 points!* The counselors who volunteered knew it was all in fun and no one was humiliated.

🐍 🐍 🐍 🐍 🐍 🐍 🐍

Day Camp Themes and Logos

"I will not venture to speak of anything except what Christ has wrought through me … by the power of the Holy Spirit." – Romans 15:18-19 RSV

In the early years of planning, we needed to come up with logos to use on brochures and tee shirts. Jim Bowser (who was one of our Fifth Quarter teens) was looking for a job as a graphic artist, and we suggested he apply at a local sports attire company that had done some silk screening for us. He got the job and is credited for most of our original camp logos which we use to this day. One of the camp logos was our marvelous *Mountain Doo Dayz* logo which came from the original artwork that Dean Whitney did for our earlier prom alternatives.

I cannot overemphasize the Lord's hand in the creation of every aspect in our day camp programming. During our first years of camp, Jim and I would go south during spring break for a week's vacation in Fairfield Glade in Crossville, Tennessee. It became our home away from home all these years. Much of my writing both for camp and my memoirs has been done at the Glade, and it is less than one hundred miles from the mountains we so love.

Over a period of more than thirty-five years, Jim and I have spent at least one week a year, sometimes two, in this beautiful serene part of the south. This amazing setting allowed God to speak to my heart as I attempted to write programming for day camp.

Our vacations to the Smoky Mountains contributed to our building of two of our four camp themes: *Indian Summer Day* activities were developed from information acquired in Cherokee, N.C. just south of the Smokies. We studied the Native American culture of Cherokee Nation and applied much of what we learned. *Mountain Doo Dayz*, with a hillbilly theme, was incorporated as one of our themes because of our love and experiences in the Smoky Mountains and our knowledge of the hill country culture.

Year after year, you could find me sitting on the deck of the timeshare we stayed at, writing as the ideas assembled together. We were amazed as the programming would develop before our very eyes. I took all the information for that summer's theme: ideas for crafts, nature lessons, Bible lessons, theme-related activities, and afternoon game ideas. I didn't have a computer at the time, so I wrote everything in free hand. We prayed and asked God to put it altogether.

At times I would get so excited that I would call Jim to come and listen as each revelation pulled the program theme together. To this day, I cannot tell you what this experience has meant to us. Praying and asking and then seeing with our own eyes what God had put down on paper. *"Ask and you shall receive, that your joy may be complete."*

There in Tennessee on warm spring days, we experienced much joy!

We have always been in awe at the creative, timeless themes God has given Five Pines. I truly believe this statement by Warren Wiersbe: *"Ministry takes place when Divine resources meet human needs through loving channels to the glory of God."* We experienced it year after year. Neither Jim nor I had a college degree or any previous training in children's programming. I personally never had the opportunity to attend camp as a child. I really didn't have any idea what a camper did at a summer camp – but God did.

Paul wrote in 2 Corinthians 3:5: *"Not that we are competent in ourselves to claim anything for ourselves, but our competence comes from God."*

God had blessed us with creative minds and the uncanny ability to create something out of whatever we had (or what someone had given us). I had previously prayed: "God give me the mind of a child playing out in the woods. Give our campers the opportunity to pretend about stepping into the adventures of the past." I soon learned that you have the attention of a child when you pretend along with them. Whether we are doing Goofy Golf, Trek West, or digging for dinosaur bones during Dino Digs, that would be the key! Pretend and it becomes almost real to them! (Even as I write this at the age of seventy-five, I still adhere to that principle.)

More than once Jim just shook his head doubting something would work out, but I believed God supplied us with everything we needed for a purpose. God gave us the desire to see what we needed and provided not only the material but the ability to successfully accomplish the use of it. Day Camp programming was indeed a gift from God.

The day camp programming afforded me one of the largest challenges and also one of the most remarkable times in my life. Each year those "creative juices" took on a new level that I had never experienced in my life. I once read a statement by the famous singer, Tony Bennett: *"The key to keeping your creativity going is to be true to yourself."* Even though I had no basis on what to rely on for ideas, I had to trust that God would take all that He had created within me and use it to bring honor to Him.

We wanted our campers to be challenged, experience God's creation in nature, and learn to love God's Word. It was definitely important to have lots of fun, but more importantly was our goal to introduce every camper to Jesus Christ.

ဒ ဒ ဒ ဒ ဒ ဒ ဒ

First Colorful Thread of Day Camp Woven

Our first full week of day camp was very successful. Kids loved it and parents were pleased. We had a most rewarding time with some excited third and fourth graders. Our campers memorized Scripture, interacted with our Bible stories, and were thrilled with the crafts they made. But our third and fourth graders had younger siblings, and they wanted to come to camp too.

Because everything went so well, we felt that the Lord wanted us to be bold and offer a full week for first and second graders and maybe *two* weeks for the third and fourth grade age (since the first year filled up to our expectations). This would stretch us some – or so we thought. By the time we were two years into our day camp program, though, we were getting more confident to offer this type of camping program to the first through fourth grade.

Year after year we would have to create a different program for a variety of ages. How were we going to continually come up with new ideas? We had no background in children's ministry and certainly very little experience. We would have to learn as we go, trust God's leading, and go the extra mile to guarantee that every program would please God.

Basically we settled into four different summer camp themes for grades one through four, on a four-year rotation:

Our silly hillbilly theme of *Mountain Doo Dayz* finds our counselors all dressed up with colorful patches on their overalls in hillbilly fashion and big black felt hats with a ole' coon tail swing'n in the breeze. It will be an entire week of crazy liv'n in them thar' hills with campers challenged to a game of Goofy Golf with walnuts and golf clubs made by my late father out of yardsticks. Campers jest luv it. Country Cook'n in the archery range is about stir'n up some opossum stew. The Ten Commandments is our Bible teaching theme and Scripture memory of Psalm 119:33-37.

Knights in Shining Armor is the exciting camp theme which draws our young knights into a medieval atmosphere as they storm a castle to rescue stolen jewels and trek through the woods of our 30 acre camp to spy on five different kingdoms. Our young squires are to solve the

144

mystery of how each king rules his kingdom. Then finally find the Kingdom of Love where the King loved his people so much he was willing to die for them. In this theme we challenge our young squires to memorize and understand the Armor of God in the sixth chapter of Ephesians.

Gold Rush Days brings on adventures of the old West and the rush for gold. Excitement surrounds the enthusiasm of our young prospectors as they Trek West to California, or pan for those sparkling gold nuggets on our big ole' sluice. Psalm 1 is the basis of our Bible lessons as well as our Scripture memory work. Our young campers are challenged to live a life pleasing to God in understanding the contrasting life of the ungodly and the Godly person.

Our fourth day camp theme in our four-year rotation was *Indian Summer Days*. It was a theme of ancient findings: the Dino Dig of buried bones, hidden trails in search of water, and the wonderful revelation of God's creative power in Genesis chapter one on creation. Some years ago, I was challenged to include a lesson entitled *Fearfully and Wonderfully Made*. It is a nature lesson on God's wonderful creation of a baby in the womb. When my daughter, Tanya, (who has a nursing degree) sat down to write this lesson, we did not cover conception or birth. We focused on those wonderful nine months in the mother's womb. The lesson was taught by a person in the medical field and has been extremely well received. Scripture memory for this theme is Psalm 19:1-4a and Psalm 139 verses 13-14. (This year we will be making some changes in the title and theme of this camp but keep the Creation/discovery focus).

I firmly believe God sends people into ministry and *equips* them to do all that He calls them to do. Of course there may be times of doubt. But we shouldn't be surprised when God provides all that we need to accomplish the task before us. I believe God wants us to use the talent He gives us. If He gives you a desire, He will fulfill it and add other people who will enrich the ministry. We decided early on that we would have to be people of "Big Faith"!

TWENTY–TWO

Different Threads of Camp Added

"With man this is impossible, but not with God; all things are possible with God."
– Mark 10:27

AS THE POPULARITY of our camps grew, in 1989 we added a week of urban camp. It was funded by a Whirlpool Corporation grant, but after two years we had to abandon that camp. Our regular camps were filling up with waiting lists, and our source for obtaining children for the urban camp was not consistently able to get the campers for their week: also the funding was no longer available.

ꙅ ꙅ ꙅ ꙅ ꙅ ꙅ ꙅ

Adventure Camp and High Adventure Camp

After many of our campers completed fourth grade camp, they expressed a desire to continue their camping experience at Five Pines, so we began an Adventure Camp for fifth and sixth grade students.

In 1991 we added another week of more advanced programming by initiating a seventh and eighth grade High Adventure Camp. This of course brought us into the situation of doing a totally different, more challenging program format for the older campers. We kept the same Bible theme for all camps but changed the theme names and still tied the younger camps and the Adventure camp themes together. So as we prepared lessons on Creation for our younger camps, we could also use the same Bible teaching theme on a higher level for our *Soaring High* adventure camp.

Here's how it worked:

First – Fourth Grade Theme	Bible Lesson	Fifth – Eighth Grade Theme
Indian Summer Days	Creation Psalm 19:1-4	Soaring High
Mountain Doo Dayz	Ten Commandments	Chart Your Course
Gold Rush Days	Psalm 1	Run the Race
Knights in Shining Armor	Ephesians 6:10-18	Army of the ONE

With this plan in place we have been able to rotate our themes every four years. It gave us the opportunity to focus on a major Bible lesson and recreate an exciting age-appropriate experience. Therefore if a camper attended Five Pines Camp for eight years, he or she would never be bored with a duplicate theme. Our main Biblical themes were still taught to all ages.

This program plan allowed our staff to plan ahead, recycle all the great material and props we had at our disposal, and easily improve what we did four years previously.

In the twenty-five years of Summer Day Camp, the schedule has changed very little. If it worked well, the programming could change, but the schedule has been much the same. Adjustments were made when we went from twenty-five campers to seventy-five campers to 120 campers per week, but that basic schedule worked.

ৡ ৡ ৡ ৡ ৡ ৡ ৡ

Camps Grow By Leaps and Bounds

"I am the vine; you are the branches. If you remain in me and I in you, you will bear much fruit; apart from me you can do nothing." – John 15:5

By 1999, five out of seven weeks of camp were 95% full with one hundred campers per week and waiting lists for some ages. Our Adventure Camps for fifth and sixth grade and seventh and eighth grade also exploded in attendance. In 2001 total enrollment for all camps soared to 693 campers. Waiting lists became the norm. Our Bible teacher, Jim Wing, continued to challenge our campers with their relationship with Christ, and an average of one hundred campers a summer responded to open their hearts to Christ.

In our first summer of camp, I remember having a total of sixty campers a week and thinking that was a full camp. But my husband kept saying we needed to take more campers, and he didn't want to have any waiting lists. When we increased to eighty-five campers per week as the maximum, we soon realized there was a demand to push our enrollment to one hundred per week. How were we going to teach five craft classes to twenty kids every half hour? (God wasn't done with growing the camps either!) The number of campers finally capped off at 120 per week as we enlarged our camps to six groups of twenty campers and four counselors per group. With God everything is possible.

We had gone from one week, to three weeks, to four weeks, to six weeks. When we added Adventure Camps, we went to eight full weeks of camp a summer. In 2003, we hit a high in enrollment of seven hundred campers with one hundred decisions to follow Christ.

The Adventure Camps challenged us to implement programs that would really stretch our fifth and sixth grade campers and even more challenging programs for our seventh and eighth graders of High Adventure.

With the addition of a high ropes course, canoeing down the

Dowagiac River, and eventually a climbing tower, we had upgraded our programming to indeed to fulfill the Adventure Camp challenge.

In addition to our on-campus programming for High Adventure Camp, in 2001 we offered two off-campus weeks of camp. One was a week-long canoe trip down the Pere Marquette River for girls and another was a boy's mountain bike trip through the Manistee National Forest.

Another year we let the High Adventure campers experience a full-day canoe trip down the Dowagiac River and an evening meal cookout where they shared stories of their adventure.

Our staff hoped to encourage the middle school students to sign up and experience one of three exciting Summit Bound trips: backpacking/whitewater rafting during spring break to the Smoky Mountains, canoeing through the Boundary Waters in northern Minnesota, or enjoying a Leelanau Peninsula road bike trip.

In 1998, we were able to advertise a whitewater rafting experience in our day camp brochure for our High Adventure campers. The city of South Bend, Indiana, offered a rafting experience on their East Race waterway. We knew our seventh and eighth campers would love a trip down the rapids. It was open to the public on Thursday nights, and the cost was only a dollar a person for about ten minutes of thrilling fun down the rapids.

Wow! This was indeed a gift to our High Adventure Camp programming. The ministry owned a bus, so we could easily take the campers down for the evening. Every year our bus was filled with campers who were certainly at an unbelievable high level of excitement.

I don't believe I've ever seen so much excitement. The rapids were indeed challenging. In fact, the United States Olympic kayaking team had used the course for practice. The six-man rafts were filled with our campers and a staff person. The rapids were wide open, and I ran the course with a camera and snapped those seconds of swirling water and campers with big eyes and lots of laughter. Once in awhile, a raft would dump all the participants in the water, but the experience was safe with lifeguards on each side all the way down.

After a few years the price went up (still reasonable), but the East Race was only open on the weekends. We used the East Race experience for about ten years, and this was one of the best (and cheapest!) activities we ever added to our camps. We felt so sorry to have to eliminate the activity – and so did the campers.

Providing a camp for the middle school students was important. It is the formable age and sometimes an age which is difficult to motivate. The experience of four years of Adventure Camp is a strategic time of character building in these campers' lives. It also encouraged many former campers to sign up to be a counselor when they got into high school.

This is one example of what a camp for this age accomplished in one young man's life. We received the following email from his teacher:

"For the past two years one of my students has attended your summer camp. I give thanks for all God is working through your efforts. You see, since this child was in kindergarten, he has missed at least one day of school per week because of parental indifference. He has been chronically late with completing assignments. But this year is different. He's had minimal absences and has completed his work on time and it's quality work. When I spoke to his mother this week, I mentioned the change. She says that he wants to be a counselor next year at your Five Pines and was told that he needed to keep his grades up to be considered for the job. This is his motivation; and it's motivating mom too. Thank you for your part in answering many years of prayers for this young man."

What an important message to our staff to be sensitive to every young camper and the family (or lack of family) and how it affects the child at this age.

🐿 🐿 🐿 🐿 🐿 🐿 🐿

Kinder Kamp

In 2004, we decided to offer an additional week of camp to those children just going into kindergarten. Some of our families expressed that younger siblings were anxious to come to camp when their older brothers and sisters came. We again stepped out in faith, trusted God, and began a new program for preschool campers. Kinder Kamp became a half-day program with a limit of sixteen campers, four counselors, and four sessions each day.

Our Kinder Kamp would run simultaneously with our other camps but have its own instructors, themes, and areas to meet in. These younger campers experienced the same but modified schedule of nature, Bible, crafts, games, and just two sessions per week in the pool. It turned out to be very successful, and there have been years when enrollment exceeded the sixteen campers. We now offer two different weeks of Kinder Kamp. God blesses in abundance.

God has also blessed Five Pines over the years with a total volunteer staff for Kinder Kamp. Jim and Jane Markle, Karen and Holly Slattery, and Sharon Fedoruk have loved on these young Kinder Kampers for years. What a remarkable group of loving Christians.

Kinder Kamp rotates the following two themes:

Themes	Bible Lesson and Scripture Memory
Krickets	*"Sing Unto the Lord"* – Psalm 96:1 and 4
Bees	*"Let every creature praise His holy name."* – Psalm 145:21

The Kinder Kamp program is run simultaneously for two of the weeks of first through fourth grade camps. More than once I felt that combining camps was too difficult to do, but it is amazing what can be done when the Lord is in it. Kinder Kamp was a great idea because we fulfilled the desire of the younger brothers and sisters who wanted to also come to camp. Each of these younger campers became seed for future years at Five Pines summer camp.

Five Pines Summer Day Camp program focused on the school age child from Kindergarten age through twelfth grade. Five Pines offers two weeks of Kinder Kamp, and eight weeks of first through eighth grade camp. In addition we offer our counselor program for ninth grade through college. Each program is highly structured, focusing on challenging each young person in a growing relationship with Christ.

How can we measure the success of six or eight weeks of camp? By the numbers, by the great time all of the campers had, by the performance of the staff, or by the program or the facilities? Although all of these things are important, success is ultimately measured by the eternal values of what God has done in the hearts of our campers.

When we look back and realize how much Scripture our campers have committed to memory, with sign language, in their eight years of their involvement at Five Pines summer day camp, it is phenomenal. All of Psalm One on the Godly and Ungodly; Ephesians 6:10-18, the Armor of God; Psalm 119:33-37 following God's Commandments and Psalm 19:1-4 on God's marvelous creation."

"... so is my word that goes out from my mouth: It will not return to me empty, but will accomplish what I desire and achieve the purpose for which I sent it." – Isaiah 55:11

For over twenty-five years, Five Pines has focused its day camp program on giving every camper, no matter what age, a total experience in programming. From the moment they stepped out of their car on Monday morning, until they sang their last song at closing on Friday, they had been part of a very dynamic week.

God and God alone brought the Five Pines camping program from us knowing absolutely *nothing* about implementing a weeklong camp to successfully running eight weeks of camp for a variety of ages. He brought us the people, the ideas, the materials, and the desire to make Five Pines camp one of the best. To God be the glory!

Harv said, "Be different than other camps and offer a unique experience. Use all the land you have. Be creative, energetic, and faithful to the Lord. Never bore a camper while you teach from God's Word and teach God's Word." Hopefully we have been faithful to Harv and to the Lord in honoring both with our day camp programs.

ภ ภ ภ ภ ภ ภ ภ

Out of the Mouths of Campers

Each day was a new adventure at camp; we never knew what was going on in their young minds or what was going to come out of their mouths. Here are just a few *"jewels"* of their expressions:

"One day I disobeyed my Dad and he was going to spank me. So I quickly asked Jesus to be my Savior."

A young camper once said, *"I wish camp went from Monday to Saturday. Then we could call it 'Six Pines!'"*

After Bible lesson about young Josiah finding the Book of the Law, the campers were to find a bag of Oreo Cookies hidden somewhere in the classroom. Jim, the Bible teacher, explained that an Oreo is like the Bible, it's what's inside that is best. One camper commented; *"We just ate the whole Bible. We know everything!"*

Prayer is part of the Armor of God but there is no armor piece that is an example of prayer. Camper: *How about the kneepads of prayer?*

Girl reading from Genesis 1:26 *"Then God said 'Let us make man in our imagination…"*

During archery: *"Powerful arm, huh?" "I got all six in the grass!"*

Camper after being told that closing ceremonies was next: *"Can't you give me detention or something so I can stay longer."*

TWENTY-THREE

The Inter-Weaving of Counselors

"Train a child in the way he should go, and when he is old he will not turn from it."
— Proverbs 22:6

IN THE BEGINNING OF DAY CAMP, our Fifth Quarter teens were more than eager to take on the responsibility of being counselors for a group of younger children. Parents were so very pleased with what we were offering, and the campers loved it. By 1987, we had 110 campers participating in our summer day camp program. As our camps grew, we needed to reach out and incorporate more teens to be counselors. Now we were challenged to step into another focus of our ministry.

We knew that we needed to develop an intense counselor orientation. Not only would our orientation train our young counselors for camp, but also challenge them to grow in *their* faith and *their* walk with the Lord. It would also be a great time for them to interact with other young people their age.

Jim Wing was a great person to set up a schedule of events and the subjects we would be covering. He also had such a great rapport with the young counselors. Our orientation served to demonstrate that we were doing a marvelous ministry to thirty to forty young people as well as being able to use them with our campers.

In the beginning we just held a three-day orientation. Then it was expanded to a week as our camps grew, our counselor numbers grew, and we added more activities to the schedule.

When the state of Michigan licensed us as a summer camp, we also had to acknowledge to the state that we were training a required number of hours of counselor and staff orientation. There were laws we had to maintain, counselor / camper ratios to be aware of, and child protection laws (just to mention a few).

A week of counselor orientation required a lot from our counselors, but it was worth it. The formal dinner, commissioning service, and foot washing ceremony were the highlights of the week creating memories to last a lifetime.

Our SONIC *(Sold Out N'In Christ)* or senior counselors, are required to counsel all age groups of campers, and participate in leadership roles during counselor orientation. Five Pines asks these young leaders to build strong relationships by mentoring and training counselors assigned to their group. We also ask them to actively engage with the parents of their campers on a daily basis.

Our counselor program has made a great impact in the lives of countless young people. Many former counselors have commented on the growth in their spiritual lives while volunteering as counselors at Five Pines. They expressed that being challenged in three areas was extremely helpful: learning and understanding Scripture daily, realizing the value of prayer, and experiencing the dependency of the Lord to accomplish each day's task.

God asked each counselor to love every child no matter how challenging. This was indeed a growing experience in their lives, giving challenges to the Lord and then seeing Him accomplish great and mighty things. They saw themselves stretched and witnessed what God was doing in ministry and in their lives. Each year, as the summer progressed, our counselors grew into a tight-knit group. In many cases they continued with their deep relationships into adulthood; rooming together at college and attending or standing up at each other's weddings. God accomplished some mighty great things in their lives, and they deeply valued the relationships they had formed.

Our prayer is that God would continue to do amazing things with all our young people who have passed through Five Pines' counselor programs.

𐤔 𐤔 𐤔 𐤔 𐤔 𐤔 𐤔

Jim Wing – A Dynamic Man of God

"But blessed is the man who trusts in the Lord, whose confidence is in him." –
Jeremiah 17:7

In 1989, Jim Wing a youth pastor from First Baptist Church in Niles, Michigan, brought his youth group to counsel the urban city camps one summer. He was a wonderful leader, and his young people were dedicated counselors. Jim and I loved how Pastor Wing interacted with his students and also how he ministered to the campers. After two years of watching Jim in ministry, we asked him to consider coming on staff as a Youth Ministry Director at Five Pines. He would be the first person on staff besides Jim and me. It was a big step in trust on both of our parts.

The following are Jim Wing's thoughts about the big step of faith he and his wife, Jeanne, were contemplating:

Some of my youth group members were counseling at an inner-city camp week at Five Pines one summer. God worked in a powerful way in some of the campers' lives, but I might say He worked in an even greater way in the lives of the counselors – and mine as well.

When it was time to make a job change, God opened the door in September of 1991 for me to join the staff at Five Pines as Youth Ministry Director. My wife and I had to raise financial support to cover half of my salary, and we worked for quite a few months to accomplish that goal. We were still short with only a couple months to go, when God supplied in an amazing way.

On a summer day, a friend of ours called us and said he'd like to come over. He had received an insurance settlement check from a car accident, and he gave us the tithe amount from that check. It was the exact amount we were short in our support! That gift gave us more time to reach our support goal and allowed me to start work at Five Pines on time with full support.

Over the next fifteen years, I was privileged to serve God in the following ways: on snowy, frigid tubing hills, belaying kids up a climbing wall and preparing them for the thrill of our zip line, teaching Bible at summer camp, leading teens in worship every Saturday night at "Five Pines Live", driving tractors for hay rides, vacuuming carpeted floors, scrubbing toilets, and washing dishes. Serving God means all those things, and that was taught and modeled at Five Pines.

Jim joined our full-time staff and was indeed a strong asset to our ministry. He was a godly man who knew the Word and was creative in presenting it.

He had a strong desire for each camper to know Christ. He consistently challenged the counselors to pray for their campers and their relationship with Jesus Christ.

Each week on Wednesday after camp, the counselors would get down on their knees and pray at each chair where a camper would be sitting on Thursday morning in Bible. (This practice of prayer has continued to this day.) Thursday's Bible lesson would be a challenge to the campers to personally know Jesus as their Savior. He also challenged our staff to pray and believe that God's movement in our lives demanded our serving Him in prayer.

One year Jim prayed that the whole camp would come forward and give their lives to the Lord – and they did. Each camper either expressed their relationship with Christ already, or their desire to now confess their sin and have a personal relationship with Christ.

We saw so many miracles during Bible in the years that Jim Wing was here and taught Bible at camp. He knew how to challenge the young campers, the counselors, as well as those in their teens at Adventure Camp.

God continued to move in our camps, and the attendance grew. We were continually challenged and moved by God's provisions.

Early on in our day camp programming, our talented Jim Wing wrote this song for our *Mountain Doo Dayz* hillbilly theme camp (and we still use it today):

Five Pines Mountain Doo Song

Lyrics by Jim Wing

Sung to the theme song of "The Beverly Hillbillies"

Let me tell y'all a story 'bout a camp Five Pines

The kin folk say as a camp it's mighty fine
There's hootin' and a-hollerin and fun fer everyone
And campers tuckered out when the week is finally done

Well the first thing you know the ce-ment pond is full
A-splashin' and a-laughin' with the campers stayin' cool
And craft-time critters will really make you grin
It's wun-ner-ful to take 'em home and show to all yore kin

Now the hound dawg Josey is the camper's best friend
His breath kinda smells but he's faithful to the end
And when it's time fer vittles thar's one thing garn-teed
Josey's thar to hep with any food that you don't need

Now thar really wuz a ser'us side in Bible class each day
We learnt the Ten Commandments and to love God and obey
The Good Book sez we all have sinned but we are saved by
grace
By trusting in a Savior, He's the Life, the Truth, the Way
Jesus, that is ..... God's only Son ..... the Holy One

This was indeed a special addition to our programming that
we all love. He also wrote the official Five Pines camp song:

Five Pines Camp Song
Lyrics by Jim Wing
Sung to the tune of "Home on the Range"

Oh… give me a camp where the weather's not damp
And the campers want piggy back rides.
Where arrows fly straight and the camp food tastes great
And all day long God's glorified
Home, home at Five Pines where the swimming pool water is
fine
Where Josey runs free and the mosquitoes bite me

But I'll praise the Lord all the day long

Jim was with Five Pines for fifteen years and then felt the Lord was leading him back to his home church as its pastor. Jim is a talented, dedicated man who gave his all to Five Pines and continued his desire to be used by God at First Baptist for the next ten years. We will always be grateful for the talent and love for the Lord Jim exemplified to everyone involved with Five Pines.

Pastor Jim was used in a mighty way, and his desire to bring campers and counselors to the Lord was blessed by God through the lives of so many young people. Here are a few camper comments from our 1998 newsletter:

"Every week I come here, I realize the wrong things I do at school. I'm glad God gives us a second chance."

"Every year I come to Five Pines, I get closer to God. It's like climbing the wall. Each step up the wall is like each year at camp."

"This is my fifth year at Five Pines, and I thought I was a Christian when I first came here. But last year I accepted Jesus as my Savior."

Our counselors and staff have endured many long, hot camp days, difficult campers, homesick campers on overnights, and campers draining every bit of energy they had. But those camper testimonies make it all worthwhile.

๑ ๑ ๑ ๑ ๑ ๑ ๑

Testimonies by Two Former SONIC Counselors

Michael Brooks: Years of Inspiration: The Impact That Five Pines Camp Has Made on Me.

The power of the Holy Spirit reverberated throughout the dim lit room, and I could hear whispered prayers echoing from within the circle of chairs. In the middle of the room sat a larger chair than the rest, with a plastic tub of water directly in front of it. As the Casting Crowns song "Your Love is Extravagant" gently played on the overhead speakers, our group took turns washing each other's feet. Virtually everyone in the room was crying, as we thanked God for one another and asked Him to bless our upcoming summer. These people were my best friends in the world, my brothers and sisters. Some I had known for years, while others I had met only two days ago. In that specific moment, I remembered thinking that no relationship I have ever had compares to those with Jesus Christ at the center.

This foot washing ceremony took place during one of my years at counselor orientation for Five Pines. Over the years this camp has remained an enormous inspiration to me, making a positive impact on my life for Christ. Time and time again, this place drew me closer to God, allowing me to experience life through His Holy Spirit.

I started attending 5 Pines going into the first grade, after my parents heard about the camp from our next door neighbor. As a child who spent a lot of time indoors, I found my six- year-old self fascinated by the immense forests and trails, and I came to love everything about the camp. So I returned each year.

As I grew up, I took part in the Adventure Camp, programs designed for older children. Along with teaching me how to have a more personal relationship with Christ, these programs provided me with leadership and teambuilding skills that I would use later in life. Campers canoed, rock-climbed, participated in team-building activities, and learned to overcome their fears suspended up in the High Ropes Course. My final year of Adventure Camp, going into the eighth grade helped me build friendships that would last years later.

Nine months later, I signed up to be a counselor at Five Pines. I always admired my counselors growing up, especially that eighth grade year, and I thought it would be a fun way to get some volunteer opportunities in for when I applied to colleges. However, at this point, I failed to see the bigger picture, that counseling wasn't about hanging out with kids, but rather teaching them about Christ in an environment where they could have all kinds of outdoor adventures.

After filling out a long and detailed application, I went in for an interview with the director of the camp. He asked me a lot of questions about my faith, most of which I couldn't answer, because my faith wasn't as strong back then. He was encouraging though, and he told me that counselor orientation would help me grow in my faith.

Around this time, I had a friend who was strong in her faith, a counselor at Five Pines already. While we were talking one day, the subject of music came up, and she asked me who some of my favorite Christian artists were. When I told her that I really didn't know any, she suggested that I look into it and even gave me a list of artists she thought I might like. At first, this thought made me laugh. For the last five years, I took weekly guitar lessons. My teacher showed me how to "rock out" to some of the best mainstream artists in secular music, and I assumed that Christian music meant loud Gospel choirs accompanying pipe organs with grand "Hallelujahs." Though I had my doubts at first, I eventually listened to this new music, following the counsel of a friend older and wiser than I.

This one bit of advice from a Five Pines volunteer changed my entire life. This new music was different from any secular music I ever heard. The songs had opposite messages than the shallow lies of the world, displaying the hope of never being alone and a close walk with Jesus Christ. Because of this music and other influences in my life at the time, I chose to recommit my life to Christ just before my first ever counselor orientation at Five Pines.

Going into my freshman counselor orientation, I was still immature in my faith, but Five Pines gave me some great role models to look up to. One of those role models made a huge impact on my life. He played the guitar for camp, and after seeing his passion for worship, his desire to give God the glory with his guitar, and not to himself, made me strive to learn worship music, and I became the leader of our Youth Group's worship band.

After counselor orientation that year, I counseled for one week. There, I saw that ordinary teenagers could make lasting impacts on the lives of children for Christh. , and I came back to counsel every year thereafter. Over the years as a counselor, I helped kids make first time salvation decisions and recommitments to their faith in Jesus. The relationships with the friends I made strengthened, and I felt again the same wonder of God's beauty in nature as when I was six years old. Being a counselor, as our director likes to say, isn't about counseling, but about discipleship, and I learned so much more about Christ while teaching kids about Him at the same time. As a SONIC or senior counselor God used my life to influence the lives of campers and the lives of younger counselors.

Every day that summer, I woke up, knowing I was doing God's will. I felt His Holy Spirit consume me, and an unquenchable fire began to burn in my heart. Because of camp, I was living out ministry every day, affecting someone else's life. Whether it was playing basketball with a camper, leading worship for the camp with my guitar, or sitting down and talking about God's love to someone, everything I did had the passion and love of the Holy Spirit behind it. As a SONIC counselor, I got to interact more with parents, and I saw how Five Pines had a "ripple-effect" on people. Kids would tell their parents about Christ, parents would start going to church, and family bonds would strengthen.

Five Pines enabled me to be the person I am today. As a child, this camp showed me the beauty of God in creation. As a preteen, it gave me an adventure to look forward to and role models to follow after. As a teenager, it enabled me to do ministry, all along the way. Five Pines gave me lasting friendships in Jesus Christ, people who I would take a bullet for and who I know would do the same for me. Five Pines strengthened my faith in the Lord, molding me from an insecure believer into an ardent defender of the faith that keeps me rooted in truth and integrity. Memories of Five Pines give me the confidence I need today to talk my non-Christian friends about Jesus and the cross.

Michael Brooks

Michael Brooks understands that his deepest identity is as God's adopted son. After college, he spent some time out west as a wilderness guide for a Christian organization, using many of the things he learned at Five Pines. He led troubled teens through the mountains of Wyoming while telling them about the hope and freedom found in Jesus Christ. Today he works as a writer for a Christian organization that uses creative art to reach the millennial generation with the

Gospel. He is a singer/songwriter, making music under the name "M Brooks" to reach listeners for Christ.

Tim Zebel: A World Changer Testimony – March 27, 2014

23 years ago, I began what would become one of the most meaningful and profound relationships in my life.

I dropped my lunch off in Maple Glen, donned a colorful button, and prepared for my first day of camp at Five Pines. At that time, the Carriage House was considerably smaller, and was known as Maple Glen. There was no craft cottage, pavilion, high ropes course or Goliath the Giant. Even so, to me this was the best place on earth. Maybe that is why I refused to leave.

After graduating as a camper, I served as a camp counselor at Five Pines for six years and as a staff member for 2 or 3 years.

I cannot overstate the impact Five Pines had in my personal development. Of course it was not just the facilities and the opportunities that Five Pines provided; it was the staff members, especially Jim Wing. Each year during the application interview he would ask what my goals were for the summer. Each year I had the same goal – I wanted to come further out of my shell and really connect with the campers. At that time I was a stoic introvert.

Every year, Jim Wing would encourage, counsel, challenge, and hold me accountable to my goal until I had so thrown off my shell that I was getting into trouble with the staff for setting new camp fads and for being too extreme.

Five Pines helped to stretch me and to provide a safe environment to practice this stretching. Throughout high school, Five Pines was a safe zone for me as I strove to grow personally and spiritually. The Five Pines Live program on Saturday nights helped to mold me into the person I am today.

I felt convinced that God wanted me to serve my sixth year as counselor and that would have left me with no money earned for Bible College. It was at this time that I was in Scofield's garage for woodworking with my camp group that Jim and I started talking about my future. Jim suggested I apply to be on paid staff as a facilitator for the MAX Challenge program.

I didn't feel it would be the right job for me. I myself am a problem solver; I'm constantly evaluating things and determining how they could be improved. Furthermore, I love to talk and share my opinions. Besides, I don't like to be cold, wet or dirty.

My job as a facilitator would require me that I would be trying to teach school groups by giving them challenges to solve and I couldn't provide them with the answers. Moreover, I'd try to use the experiences of these challenges to teach these groups, but I could only ask questions to accomplish this.

Honestly, I didn't think I could sit and watch a group struggle without helping them. In fact, I learned later that pretty much the entire staff at Five Pines agreed with me and told Jim that I couldn't do this job.

But Mr. Scofield had faith in me and I agreed to take the job. Well he was right, I could do the job and I loved it. It was outside my comfort zone, but God is faithful to equip us to accomplish what He has called us to do.

My heart had been with the short term mission trips as a Bible currier in Asia. I had been doing this since I was 17yers old. Five Pines was aware of my desire and one summer I felt drawn to a ministry in Asia. Five Pines had invested in me as a staff person but understood my desire to serve in missions. It was that summer that I decided that God wanted me to live in Asia and help a missionary with the church there.

Upon moving to a large city in Asia, I immediately began utilizing the skills that I had learned at Five Pines. Group management, the power of questions, etc, became crucial skills in my new ministry.

For years, these people had been asking for a summer camp. The pastor at the church was from the city and had no idea how to run a summer camp. But God had equipped me with my background of 8 years at Five Pines as a camper and six years as a counselor plus my staff experience.

The first year of running a camp... was pretty crazy. This camp had to be underground because it is an illegal activity. We were in the largest business city; a city of about 14 million people. Consequently, most of the activities had to be done indoors in our apartment because there were no open fields or woods.

The first year of camp did not go as we expected. But it was a huge success, the campers raved about how awesome camp was. It was unlike anything they had ever experienced. One teenage boy got saved, and years later, he attended our Bible College. After camp was finished, one of the young girls wanted to go to bed early so that she could dream that she was back at camp. God truly blessed our efforts.

The next year it grew to 40 campers. We had access to better facilities and I was able to implement my camp schedule based upon Five Pines' model. Most of the games were ones I had learned at Five Pines and I even ran a camp orientation program to train camp workers.

Our third year we had 80 campers, we even bused in campers from other churches.

So integral was my experience at Five Pines to the integrity of our camp that I can honestly say that Five Pines has gone international. The church I served in Asia had 300 people, and ran 6 sub-ministries. After serving many years in Asia, my family now resides in the States.

All of this is the fruit of Jim Scofield's unmerited faith in a college kid and Five Pines staff's willingness to train him. Of course, Five Pine's was not intending to build up a future missionary who would extend camp ministry to another country, but God was. It is in this way that Five Pines truly is building an unsung army of world changers.

Tim Zebel

Tim Zebel is presently a writer with Foreunners Of America. FOA is an organization which goal is to help empower Christians to speak into cultural issues with an influential and relevant voice.

TWENTY-FOUR

MAX Course – Maximum Adventure Xperience

BACK IN 1989, Don Gast introduced us to another person for part-time program staff. Tim Chaddock was working at the Southwestern Medical Clinic as well as seeking his doctorate in counseling. He also had an interest in Christian camping. We were looking to add camping and programming for fifth and sixth as well as seventh and eighth grade camps. So we brought Tim on as Program Director with a challenge to develop a junior high program. One Saturday he sponsored a "Paddle and Pizza" outing, and to our surprise fifty-four junior high youths arrived. It was a great success, and with that began Tim's short but valuable time at Five Pines.

Tim was interested in outdoor programming and introduced us to our very first two challenge elements on a "high" ropes course. These would be the initial elements of our MAX Challenge program and for our new Adventure and High Adventure Camps. Our course was only about fifteen feet off the ground, but it was enough of a challenge for middle school students.

Remember David, whose life was changed through the TWA program and gave his heart to the Lord? Sometime after his death, his mother gave us a small memorial gift as she shared what Five Pines meant to David's life. Five Pines had given David some of the best years of his life. Through the input of God's Word and our programs, he had found hope for a better future. I believe he saw Jim as the father he never had. His mother asked Jim to use the gift as a memorial to David. We were just in the process of installing our first elements on the new MAX Challenge Course and she said that would have been something he would have loved to do. Thus the challenge course is named in memorial to David.

Directors Kermit and Jean Hanley invited our staff to visit Eagle Village and observe their large indoor ropes course. Of course it was way above any of our dreams or needs, but it was good to get ideas. They were wonderful people who shared a lot of their expertise in challenge programs with us.

In 1991, Tim designed a climbing and rappelling wall on the west side of our playground equipment. It was only ten-foot high, but it was a start and the campers loved it. This was our first year of High Adventure Camp, and we offered two elements on the ropes course and climbing and rappelling on the wall. Wow! We had come a long way, or so we thought. We were offering eight full weeks of camp from first through eighth grade. Unbelievable!

Tim left to go back to school but God brought Tim into the Five Pines ministry to help upgrade ideas for older campers and then let him move on. It seemed like this would often be a pattern of God working in our ministry; bring someone into our lives for a specific purpose and then move them on. When Tim left, God brought Jim Wing on staff as Youth Director, and Carter Newell came on as Summit Bound Director and Adventure Experience programming. With these two new staff people, we were able to do more advanced programming for junior and senior high campers and expand our MAX Adventure program with the schools.

Here are three objectives we established as we moved forward with the Maximum Adventure Xperience:

To provide an environment which uses experiential education to increase knowledge, develop new skills, and clarify values.

To use perceived risk activities with a "your challenge, your choice" philosophy. Allowing kids to step out of their comfort zone to increase self and group discovery.

To use challenge-based learning to encourage positive behavior and outcomes which enhance the growth of leadership development.

Our program staff worked with over 2,000 students during the spring and fall of 2002. I have no idea how God impacted the lives of those young people, but our staff prayed every morning for opportunities to be a witness. This was more of a *sowing* program, and we trusted that others would reap what our staff had sown.

One such instance occurred during a closing session when Jim Wing told the public school students about 1 Corinthians 15:33: "Don't be deceived. Bad company corrupts good character." Later a parent asked Jim, "Where is that in the Bible? I want to share that with my daughter."

Here's a great example of the immediate effect the MAX Adventure program had on one student. This is from her teacher's perspective:

"I had one girl who overcame her fear of heights. I saw a different child come home on the bus. She has since started to reach out to other students for friendship. This is now not the 'little girl' that sat silently in her room."

Thank You! Upton Middle School Teacher

ยายายายายายาย

A Gift - The Original Climbing Tower

"With your help I can advance against a troop; with my God I can scale a wall."
Psalm 18:29

In the fall of 1993, we were having all our hayride groups meet in our garage. We spent time going over the rules before our group boarded the hay wagons. In one corner of the garage, we set up a display with photos and brochures of the numerous programs offered at Five Pines. One of the photos showed a girl climbing the wall on the playground equipment from the previous High Adventure Camp.

A gentleman noticed the photo and asked, "Where do you have a climbing wall?"

Jim said, "It is only ten-foot high and on the front side of the playground equipment."

The man asked, "Would you like a *real* climbing tower? I built one for Notre Dame and know where we could get the poles. I can help you build it."

It was another God thing. Who would have thought? A man shows up for a hayride, sees the display, and a conversation ensues. He provides the poles, engineers the design, and offers his expertise to help build it!

So in 1994, Jim began the unbelievable dream of building a 28-foot climbing and rappelling tower. The tower was four-sided with different degrees of difficulty on each side. The top had a rail around it and was designed for rappelling down the back side. At the time our tower was built, there weren't any regulations to follow or certifications to get. We followed the advice from other camp directors who had similar towers.

I was out of town when the men came to install the poles and build the tower. My first opinion when I drove out to see the almost completed tower was, *"You have to be kidding. Nobody is going to climb that."* Little did I know the eagerness of almost every young person who had that challenge set before them and the depth of the challenges that were met as people of all ages. Little did I see the magnitude of outreach this tower would create. Little did I realize that in twenty years, I would climb higher than the twenty-eight feet on our new tower that replaced this one!

Over the eighteen years that this tower was in use, it was an important element of the MAX challenge program. Over 20,000 students have worked through some life-changing experiences on the tower. Our staff has worked with over forty-two schools, primarily from Southwestern Michigan, with over 1,600 students per year coming to experience the MAX program. Fear of heights is common as is low self-esteem and fear of failing. Through the years we witnessed:

- Young people confined to a wheelchair because of a life- long illness, climbing the tower using just their arms.

- Two boys seemed to argue constantly and didn't get along at camp, but agreed to be tied together in a climb. They learned to help each other, encourage each other, and achieve success together – all the way to the top. Success made them friends from then on.

- Many campers were terrified and constantly wanted to quit. Through much encouragement from their peers and staff, they continued and made it to the top and rang the bell. Victories were witnessed every day.

One student, whose legs were too weak to hold himself up, began to climb and then another student climbed just under him. That second climber moved and held the first climber's feet to the footholds as they both climbed together.

In our 1998 autumn newsletter, Jim wrote this in the Director's Desk column:

One student who recently participated in the MAX Adventure Xperience program wore a T-shirt that read, **"Army of the Lord"** *on the front side and* **"Working for God is not just a job; It's an Adventure"** *on the back side. When I review the past six months in our ministry, I must certainly agree it has been an adventure.*

As I take time to think of the hundreds of students I have belayed on the tower, I can't help but think of the different personalities, struggles, and approaches to failure or success. Their needs, both emotionally and spiritually, are sometimes overwhelming. Each is an individual, created by God with an immense need for a loving and caring environment. The world tries to address these needs, but it is not doing a very good job. ("It takes a village to raise a child.") Failure seems more common than success, and giving up is easier than trying harder.

I've belayed students who were from the Student Council, Alternative Ed programs, emotionally impaired, as well as the County Juvenile Center. What a privilege to hear the director of an alternative education program say, "This program fills the hole that has been in our program for the past five years. It was tremendous!" We pray that the very short time of opportunity we have with each student will influence them in some way to re-direct their lives and eventually lead them to our Savior.

Jim Scofield

Life-changing experiences are what our MAX challenge program is all about. The staff at Five Pines has facilitated many different groups on the tower, not just students and campers:

- The ROTC from Notre Dame *(At first they were going to be flown to Five Pines in Apache helicopters and land in the field, west of the pool. Imagine what our neighbors would have thought! But the helicopters were not available to Notre Dame. They arrived in vans, not helicopters.)*
- A group of women who were part of an abuse support group *(There were many tears, but their determination was high. Their accomplishments were great. They expressed love, support, and encouragement won over.)*
- Groups of firefighters and police *(Some had fears of heights and wouldn't rappel.)*

The fruit of our harvest is not especially ours to see, but once in awhile God allows us to hear or witness what He has done through our efforts of sharing His love. The following is a testimony from one of our public school teachers:

I had a student who two years ago climbed the tower. Before we came, she didn't smile much nor did she appear to be very positive. She spent twenty minutes trying to climb the wall, and she shed many a tear in her fight to reach the top (trying to find confidence and self-determination) and the desire to come down. When we left, she thanked me and the staff for having so much faith in her and for the encouragement. This wasn't just a "school trip" for her. It was a turning point in her life; a renewal of spirit, if you will. She found confidence and courage she never thought she had. She became a more positive person and happier, which allowed her to make new friends. I not only observed this through her years at our middle school, but she made it a point to tell me how Five Pines had changed her life a year or two after her experience.

Last year this young girl's father died suddenly, and two months later her mom had a new baby. I believe God worked through Five Pines to teach her and prepare her for such a life change; He knew she needed it."

ㅂ ㅂ ㅂ ㅂ ㅂ ㅂ ㅂ

Zip Line – 1997

Each year my husband and our staff wanted to expand the elements on the Max Challenge Course, so we decided that there was enough of a hill and a deep dip at the bottom that they could build a zip line. They built a platform on the tree at the top and ran the cable down right over the tent platforms and up to an ending platform. We had a MAX school group coming the next week, and of course the staff wanted the zip line finished. They were determined to use it.

Jim kept saying it wasn't safe and we weren't going to use it. The staff was very upset because they were so determined to use it. So they tried it with a cement block attached, but the cable was too straight (not enough dip in it). Also one major thing was missing: a brake. There was nothing to stop it!

Our staff was anticipating it would dip in the low area and slow down. Then a person, who was the catcher, could grab the end of an attached rope (to be used to run the line back up the hill). Sharon, who was hired in 1995 as a school liaison, tried to hang on to the line. Well, when the cement block started to pick up speed, she continued to hold on to slow it down and stop it. As the cement block continued to go down the hill, she lost layers and layers of skin on her hands. She didn't stop the cement block. Lessons learned!

The staff more or less came back to the office with their tails between their legs, knowing full well that the zip line was not ready. They had some engineering to do.

Eventually with more adjustments, the zip line was tested and proven safe and has been used by thousands of young people and adults. It is safe, challenging, and most people would say the best thing on the MAX course.

𝕊 𝕊 𝕊 𝕊 𝕊 𝕊 𝕊

A Heart-Warming Ride Down the Zip Line

One of the most memorable "snapshots" on the the zip line occurred during a middle school outing. The students were here for a day of team building and MAX Course experiences.

One young girl, "Sandra", was part of the class and had been confined to her wheelchair all of her young life. She had a good attitude during the team building activities in the morning. In the afternoon, she sat there watching all of her fellow students experience the six elements on the high ropes course, knowing full well she couldn't do any of them. She had such a sweet spirit about her. She looked sad when it came time for many of the students to experience the zip line.

Then one of her teachers approached our staff and asked for a favor. If the teacher could get up the ladder to the deck of the zip line, could a person carry Sandra up the ladder to the deck? If so, the teacher wanted to harness Sandra to herself and take the young girl with her down the zip line.

Our staff talked it over, and someone finally said, *"We are always telling the students to take a risk and accomplish something you don't think you can do. I think it's time we challenged ourselves to do the same thing."*

I wish time could have stood still as this amazing attempt of love was played out. The hardest part was carrying Sandra up the ladder to the platform. When she took off from the platform, she was free from her constraints and flying through the air. Those six seconds gave her a thrilling experience of a lifetime. Sandra's face lit up like an angel, and her smile stayed with her the rest of the day.

There has never been anything like this since, and I'm not sure will ever play out again.

ⅶ ⅶ ⅶ ⅶ ⅶ ⅶ ⅶ

Team Building

Early in our MAX team-building program, we were able to do half of the Upton Middle School sixth grade class. In the fall, half of the class went to Chicago to visit a museum, the other half were scheduled to participate in the Five Pines MAX program. Throughout the remainder of the year, the teachers were amazed at the difference in attitudes of those who came to Five Pines and those who didn't. Since then, *all* of the sixth graders of Upton Middle School participate in the fall activity of team building and the MAX Course.

Over the years, our staff has led over 20,000 middle school students through the Maximum Adventure Xperience (including team-building initiatives, ropes course and climbing of the Tower). Our staff and the teachers have had the blessings of watching students grow in new ways. We use the method of experiential education to allow students to be challenged out of their comfort zones.

These are activities which help students grow in areas of motor, social, cognitive, and affective skills. They are building blocks for personal growth and leadership development. The unique aspect of the Five Pines MAX program is that the outdoors is used as a classroom, and fun is combined with challenge learning.

That, in itself, is very exciting. The bonus is understanding the impact that is felt on a broader scale. Teachers and parents who come to support and help chaperone the groups are impacted by the dramas that play out in front of them each day. They recognize the negative behaviors that surface during team building, but they also get to watch as those behaviors are changed in exciting ways. Their students walk away with newfound skills and confidence, and the teachers walk away refreshed and excited. They know that growth has happened in meaningful ways.

The core of the program is in the staff-directed processing that happens as students talk about their experience in small groups which reinforce the group's goals and objectives. Our staff members allow students to learn from each other and themselves in that moment.

So clearly there have been times when students are not eager to participate and challenge themselves. Here's one such instance:

Jamie (not his real name) was adamant. With a scowl on his face, his arms crossed, and no eye contact, the message he clearly sent was: *"I'm not doing anything."*

The first activity was the high ropes course. Jamie refused to put on a harness. His teacher took him for a walk and told him he needed to cooperate. He began to cry. *"I want to do it, but I can't".*

Soon the teacher persuaded Jamie to put on the harness, but he just stood there and muttered a nasty name to his teacher. As he summoned up some courage, Jamie put on the harness, completed the high ropes course, and a spark of life came to him. He then climbed our tower *twice* and rappelled, his confidence growing.

We led an affirmation time for the afternoon wrap-up session. The students took turns complimenting each other, and the teacher was asked to get in front. Jami raised his hand and, in a quiet voice, said, "Thank you for helping me this morning to be in a good mood to participate."

What difference did Five Pines make in this "at risk" junior high boy's life? One thing we *do* know: He has some really good memories of a day when he was challenged, encouraged, and accepted.

੩ ੩ ੩ ੩ ੩ ੩ ੩

Team Works!

In 1998, we established a new program for corporate development. Our purpose statement was: *"Team Works! removes the participants from the daily stress of the office and uses a natural setting and supporting atmosphere to encourage participants to explore self-imposed limits and the challenge of effective teamwork."* The outdoor tasks helped individuals become effective team members while attempting to solve group problems. God used this program in various ways with all kinds of professional organizations.

One summer, a superintendent had been looking for something different than bringing the traditional speaker in to kick off the school year. He decided he would trade the classroom for an outdoor experience. So he brought his group of teachers to spend a day at Five Pines for our *Team Works!* program. He wanted to build a better support group and establish a closer working relationship with his staff.

The date they came was August 25th. The next day, two of their young students died in an alcohol-related automobile accident, and our staff realized that their appointment with the teachers was in God's plan.

Four days later, the superintendent stopped by Five Pines and expressed that he and all the teachers dealt with the tragedy better because of the experience they had just had at Five Pines. His words were, *"You won't believe how much good it did. We need to get the juniors and the seniors out here in the next week and go through this program with them."*

The next day our staff adjusted their busy schedule and worked with the group of young students in the MAX program. The students strengthened their friendships and learned to support each other. They had overcome and become much closer as they healed together.

☒ ☒ ☒ ☒ ☒ ☒ ☒

The Tower Unravels

It was the spring of 2008. We were conducting our annual certified challenge course inspection when we heard the words: "The tower does not pass inspection." The Association of Challenge Course Technology (ACCT) had recently upgraded the standards for climbing towers. The six poles supporting the tower were old and not the required Class 2 treated utility poles. When the tower was originally built in 1994, there weren't any standards for challenge course programming. We just followed suggestions of those who were the experts of challenge programs at the time.

The tower was an integral part of our outdoor experiential education program. It was a driving force adding more value to our

MAX program and an amazing enhancement to our summer adventure camps.

This was very discouraging to see it come down and another tower not go up. But a new tower would be a big expense, and it would take a number of years to establish the design, raise the finances, clear the land, hire a contractor, and build it. We would also need to purchase all the handholds, ropes, carabineers, and harnesses.

The tower was very significant in our challenge ministry, so for several years we climbed the "Tall Trees" (actual trees) while we raised the money. I was desperate to get a new tower completed. I went to our director, Michael Holets, and boldly made this statement: "If you get the tower done, I'll be the first to climb it!"

ㅂ ㅂ ㅂ ㅂ ㅂ ㅂ ㅂ

Goliath the Giant Tower – 2010 to 2015

"A giant nearly ten feet tall stepped out from the Philistine line into the open, Goliath from Gath." – 1 Samuel 17:4 MSG

Thus our director, Michael Holets, and staff began the process of laying out desirable plans for a new tower. As our builder laid out his plans, he explained that it would be extremely sturdy and would withstand winds of ninety miles per hour. He used God's design of the honeycomb to build the 52½-foot hexagon-shaped climbing tower with five climbing or rappelling sides. It was exciting to think that this was a possibility, but the estimated cost was over $100,000. We asked the Lord to bring people and organizations to help Five Pines finance this big project.

A young man named Nathan was involved in the ministry of Five Pines as a child in our day camp program. As a high school sophomore he served as a day camp counselor. Later on in life, he was in the Navy and an accomplished midshipman. But Nathan was secretly facing the *Goliath"* of clinical depression in his life that he felt he couldn't overcome – and sadly took his life.

It was devastating to his family and the family of Five Pines. Our hearts always say, "If we only knew ..." Thus, the "Lessons of Goliath the Tower" have Nathan's struggles in mind. The tower was built to remind us of the struggles our young people face and to encourage them that *no Goliath is too big to overcome.*

Sadly another young man's life and death affected the outcome of funding to complete the climbing tower. Josh Martin went to be with the Lord in a tragic accident in 2014. It had been a deep desire of Josh, a former camper but now a young businessman, to see that Goliath was completed. Through many generous memorials to Josh, the needed funding to complete Goliath was accomplished.

In the summer and fall of 2013, construction began with the dedication on May 1, 2015. The new tower has 3,700 square feet of climbing surface and is one of the tallest in Michigan. Our staff pre-drilled 10,000 holes for possible hand holds. It is constructed with durable tongue and groove boards with outcroppings for more difficult climbs. The tower is capped off by a metal-covered deck. It is indeed a premium climbing challenge tower.

It is a desire that the new tower, "Goliath" will be an encouragement to young people facing struggles and overcoming them with a new perspective on life. It is all about developing an "I can do it" attitude.

Five Pines wants to create an atmosphere for positive change, reinforce confidence, develop leadership skills, and test values. The end result is better discussions, active learning, and mental or emotional breakthroughs. At the very least, seeds will be planted that impact the future.

With Christian groups we can base all of our teaching applications on God's Word. With public schools, we can teach the same principles but not relate them to the Word of God. (*"Someone very wise wrote this a long time ago ..."*) Those life applications, along with the power of God, teach us that all of us can overcome our fears and be courageous. What a great tool for learning the most important lessons in life. We can't ... but God can!

ㅂ ㅂ ㅂ ㅂ ㅂ ㅂ ㅂ

Meeting the Challenge - 2015

Now about the challenge that I gave myself years before: to be the first to climb Goliath. At every fundraising dinner, our director would mention the tower to our guests and add the note that I had volunteered to be the first to climb Goliath. People would laugh, and I would always respond by saying that I didn't say how high! It could be only a couple of steps, but they would have to come and see. Most of the people who were there doubted me. I even doubted if I would even *try*, and it was kind of a joke between Michael and me.

Goliath was dedicated in the spring of 2015. Michael challenged the board of directors and the people who were there at the dedication to put money down on the number of boards I would climb. I didn't want this to be a circus event but accepted the challenge if money would go to camp scholarships. As I kept climbing, and climbing, people began to think that maybe I would make it to the top. Each step I took was amazing to most of the people who were there, but I kept going.

One board member went over to Michael and asked, "How far is she going to climb? Is this going to cost me?"

Michael responded by saying, "Probably."

On May 1, 2015 at the dedication ceremony of this fine climbing tower, I kept my promise and climbed Goliath. I reached just over forty-two feet of the 52-foot climbing surface – one step at a time. Challenges are to be met. "With my God I can scale a wall." In my life, I can scale any "wall" because God is so faithful.

"For my thoughts are not your thoughts, neither are your ways my ways,' declares the Lord. 'As the heavens are higher than the earth, so are my ways higher than your ways, and my thoughts than your thoughts.'" – Isaiah 55:8-9

I had confidence in God, and the two new knee replacements I had over the previous years. My bad back was also stronger due to water therapy and exercise. I was attempting to live out the statement: "Push back against age as much as it pushes against you."

This climb would cost some people, and many had to dig deep into their pockets as I climbed higher than most thought. We raised $4,200 for camp scholarships, and it was just three days short of my seventy-fifth birthday. What a birthday present! To God be the glory!

"I can do all things through Christ who strengthens me." – Philippians 4:13 NKJV

TWENTY–FIVE

The Surprising Threads of God's Provision

"But my God shall supply all your needs according to his riches in glory by Christ Jesus." – Philippians 4:19 KJV

NAIER
National Association for the Exchange of Industrial Resources

Early in our ministry, when we first became involved in CCCA, some camping directors shared with Jim that being a member of NAIER was very profitable to their camps. NAIER enabled them to purchase a variety of things at a very nominal cost.

NAIER is basically a clearinghouse of surplus products. Jim decided to see what NAEIR was all about, so he signed up to be a member.. We would travel down to central Illinois a few times a year and load our van or a truck with an unbelievable amount of things from the "Grab Bag"; anything from windows to carpeting to craft items to pallets of commercial grade vinyl wallpaper. Belonging to NAIER was certainly an asset to this young and growing ministry.

ଯ ଯ ଯ ଯ ଯ ଯ ଯ

Crafts that Last – Indeed a Walk with God

We established early that our crafts would strongly relate to the theme of the year as well as be durable. For over thirty years, I believe we have successfully accomplished the goal of offering excellent crafts in our summer day camp programming.

Often we hear the counselors say, "I *still* have my (craft) that I made when I came to camp." They still cherish them. It's kind of silly to hear sixteen-year-olds talk about their "gold" from *Gold Rush Days* or their sword with all the jewels from *Knights in Shining Armor* or their coon tail from *Mountain Doo Dayz*. They will probably never throw away the basket or the wooden notepad they made in Adventure Camp. Good memories make for good counselors.

When we read in Exodus how God provided nourishment for His children on a daily basis, we have to sometimes remember how God provides our every need (even in this day). As I think back of the *tons* of craft materials we acquired free over the years, that supply has allowed us to offer the very best crafts to our campers year after year.

As an example, probably twenty years ago a lady who knew of our ministry was working at a place that did upholstery for golf carts. She gave us *boxes and boxes* of lightweight vinyl, scraps she had left over and would have otherwise thrown out. We have used that vinyl to sew scabbards for our Knights to attach to their belts to hold their swords. We still have enough material for another couple of years. Remarkable indeed, twenty years ago!

Then we have those large wooden beads used in forming the comfort seat cushions often seen in pickup trucks. Two huge bags of beads were donated by a local man in the wrecker business, and we use the beads in numerous crafts year after year to make wooden cross necklaces. We finally ran out of the cushions but found more online. We were glad that we could continue the great wooden bead cross necklace.

§ § § § § § §

"The Sweat Shoppe"

The Sweat Shoppe, as we have always called it, is a group of about ten volunteer ladies who help prepare the materials for crafts each year. The Sweat Shoppe meets about three times during the spring months. They are wonderful ladies who do a lot of laughing as the hours pass by. They measure, cut, and staple all the crafts needed for that year.

For our *Gold Rush Days* camp crafts, they tear the 14,000 one-inch strips of muslin needed for our young campers to make their wagon train rag dolls. One lady, and I won't mention her name, is known as our "stripper". She tears all those 1½-inch strips of muslin, one strip at a time. At the same time, other ladies are cutting out the hundreds of aprons, shawls, and scarves the girls will be using to dress their dolls *and* the denim jeans and shirts for the boy dolls. Remember we are talking about providing materials for up to three hundred campers each summer.

I also want to acknowledge Alice, my dear friend, neighbor, and right hand craft helper. Alice has been with me almost every morning of camp in the Craft Cottage from the beginning days of camp. We have tackled many challenges together, and I couldn't have done it without her. It's not easy to get twenty campers in and out of crafts every half hour and make sure their crafts are done.

One day a young boy camper made a remark to me as he exited the Craft Cottage that fits every one of these wonderful ladies: *"Some old Grandmas like you are awesome!"* A labor of love, indeed! These ladies are awesome!

ꍏ ꍏ ꍏ ꍏ ꍏ ꍏ

Real Raccoon Tails for *Mountain Doo Dayz*

I felt it was a long shot, but I thought it would be great if our campers were awarded a real fur tail for learning their memory work. It fit the theme, and we could make a binder twine belt to hang the tail on.

In the very first year of *Mountain Doo Dayz* camp (twenty-five years ago), we thought that a display of all the "hunting trophies" someone in the mountains might have shown off would be the number of animal skins from their skills. So our original thoughts were to cut up furs of different kinds.

That spring Jim and I attended a conference in Indianapolis, Indiana, and we visited a Goodwill store (during some time off) looking for a good buy on a fur coat. It was late spring, and all the fur coats were on sale for $2.00 each! We bought five of them and cut them up into fur tails when we got home. It was a *job,* and we prayed that we would find another avenue to get those fur tails!

Four years later, when we were traveling across Nebraska to see our son in Colorado, we stopped at a souvenir store. I noticed the coonskin caps with the coontails hanging down the back. They were made in Cherokee, North Carolina.

I wrote the Chamber of Commerce at Cherokee and asked them who made the souvenir hats. They informed me they were made by the Cherokee Nation. The man at the Chamber of Commerce told me to contact a lady named Kay. She ran a Native American craft store in Cherokee and could be a source of information.

Kay was a very wonderful and gracious lady who helped me secure the two hundred to three hundred coontails every four years for the last sixteen years. She purchased them from the Cherokee business, and every year I prayed that she would still be there for me.

Once I commented that the tails were getting smaller, and she said it was because of the fall of communism in Russia. The wealthy leaders in Russia were not buying as many fur coats as they used to, so there wasn't a market for the raccoon skins (and the tails were not as full either).

It is interesting how the fall of communism affected the souvenir industry of the Cherokee nation in America and also our little ministry in Southwestern Michigan. Kay also related that the turkey feathers the Cherokees used in their feathered head pieces were more difficult to get. This is because turkey farms inject hormones into the turkeys to make them grow faster, and that doesn't give them time to grow feathers. Wow! No wonder the cost for our artificial eagle feathers for *Indian Summer Days* increased.

The last time we visited Kay in her store, tourism was not picking up in Cherokee and the store closed.

Eventually we had to find a new source for our coontails, and that took us to Niagara Falls, New York, to *Chichester Furs* for our real coontails. This too was an interesting act of God. I feared that the price would be too high, and we'd have to go to another idea for an "award" for *Mountain Doo Dayz*.

God had worked it out! It was the end of May 2013, and we traveled to Boston for our granddaughter's college graduation. Niagara Falls was only about fifteen miles off the interstate. I could easily look over the coontails and purchase what I needed. God is good. They had plenty for me to choose from, and the price was *better* than what I had been paying in Cherokee! It was amazing indeed that God re-directed our paths to accomplish a needed task; something as simple as a real coontail.

☙☙☙☙☙☙

Covered Wagon

"With man this is impossible, but not with God; all things are possible with God."
– Mark 10:27

When we planned our first year of *Gold Rush Days* back in the late 1980's, I wanted to schedule a covered wagon ride for our campers to take them to the "back forty" acres to pan for gold. We had the three hay wagons, and the smaller one would make a great covered wagon – but what about the top? I kept telling Jim I wanted a covered wagon, and he looked at me like I was crazy!

We thought that we could easily bend PVC pipe from side to side to form the top framework. Then all we needed was a cover. Jim mentioned it to a friend, Earl Maxwell, who owned a local junk yard. He thought a minute and said that he had just picked up the old "cloud nine" from the local high school track program. *When we laid the white vinyl material out on the ground and measured it, it was exactly the right width and length for the wagon!* I even had enough extra to sew a section to place a drawstring through to draw up in front and in back of the wagon. It fit remarkably well.

Now this in itself sounds like a miracle match, but there is more. The "cloud nine" had a top and a bottom to it, and it was pumped with air to form a cushion for the high jump athletes to land on. Inside the double layer were straps attaching the top to the bottom to keep its shape. These straps were attached to loops on the underneath side of the top.

When we cut the top from the sides and the bottom and removed the long straps, the loops lined up *exactly* with the PVC pipe we had attached for the framework! With all this in place, we had a wonderful covered wagon that only God could have provided. This again was the continuation of many "miracles". Everything is possible for those who believe, according to Mark 9:23. Jim and I had to believe and not to set limits on what God can do.

So a few years later when we acquired a free pallet load of canvas from NAEIR, I was able to sew a new cover for the wagon which allowed the light to come through. The hay wagon is recreated into a covered wagon every two years, and is still in use today.

ㅂ ㅂ ㅂ ㅂ ㅂ ㅂ ㅂ

Craft Cottage – 1996

From the first year of day camp, we used the ski room of the Activity Center (A.C.) for our crafts. Enrollment in the day camp program was increasing every year, and in 1994 we were up to 370 campers. It was difficult to get fifteen to eighteen campers plus their counselors around the craft table (the size of a ping pong table) because the room wrapped around the main section of the Activity Center in an "L" shape.

A Christian school in nearby Niles had an abandoned portable classroom that the fire department wanted them to get rid of. They offered it to Five Pines just to get it off their property. Our friend, Earl, who was always ready to do anything for Five Pines, split it apart and hauled the two sections over to our camp.

It wasn't until 1996, though, that the Craft Cottage was completed. Jim had the building set up in an area northeast of our garage. We were over four hundred campers in summer camp now, and a "new" enlarged craft building was certainly a necessity.

The abandoned classroom was really a disaster when we first got it. It actually was falling apart! Jim and his crew replaced the rafters and built a new roof. They tore out the inside walls, installed a new floor, and dry-walled all the exterior walls. We had an odd assortment of windows from NAIER, and at this point it didn't matter whether they matched or not. They were windows and they worked! We brightened the interior with some beautiful heavy duty vinyl wallpaper and matching drapery material to cover the odd assortment of windows. All of this was from NAIER.

Also a family in our ministry remodeled their kitchen, and we eagerly accepted all their old kitchen cabinets for the new Craft Cottage. God provided us with four large old schoolroom tables for camper work stations and other tables to lay crafts on.

Later an old deck was attached to the back of the craft building. It was a bonus for drying our pottery and the beautiful baskets our Adventure Camp girls make.

The investment into this very nice craft building was probably no more $1,500, and it is a perfect place to teach crafts with lots of storage space. All of this helped make the cottage come alive for the thousands of campers who have passed through its doors with creative crafts in hand; memories that will last a lifetime.

ª ª ª ª ª ª ª

Adventure Camp Crafts

In 1996 we added a woodworking craft for the boys in fifth and sixth grade Adventure Camp. We wanted these older boys to learn some woodworking skills that probably most boys would never learn from their fathers. The crafts would be simply constructed, not costly, and yet teach a basic skill. All components would be previously cut for the young Adventure campers to assemble.

My father, Larry Rose, was a creative person who could make almost anything. So we sat down and came up with two different crafts: a Tic-Tac-Toe game and a small wooden note pad with a roll of paper. These were crafts that would teach the young boys how to measure, use a drill press, sand the wood smooth, stain the project, and assemble it.

Dad was in his late 80's and was reluctant at first to teach the crafts. But once he did he *loved* it, and the boys loved doing a man-type craft with a grandpa teaching it. Dad equipped the workshop with four drill presses. That donation enabled all the boys to keep busy with their craft. We also were grateful for the volunteers who helped the boys complete their project and instill safety using the equipment.

The Adventure Camp boys worked out of our garage, and although it always seemed somewhat of a mess to me, the boys thought it was a great workshop and seemed to take ownership of it. It was a move out of the Craft Cottage (where the girls were making baskets) to a manly workshop. It was a wise move.

After my father went to be with the Lord, Jim took over as teacher. Those wonderful Tic-Tac-Toe games and notepads are still made today. Again, we felt God continually helping us fill in the blanks when new areas opened up in ministry.

While the fifth and sixth grade boys tackled their woodworking project, the girls did basket weaving in the Craft Cottage. My daughter, Tanya, had been weaving baskets for some years. I told her my desire for the Adventure Camp girls to have a challenging craft, take the full five days of camp, and result in a very nice craft. Making a basket would meet all those criteria and be cost effective.

We found a pattern for a cute basket with a handle and included a strip of dyed reed with a reed bow. The small basket was entitled "Cookies for Two".

The basket-weaving project would require the entire reed for thirty-five baskets to be cut in advance – some of it dyed. All the baskets and reed had to be soaked each day before the girls could work on it. This too would be a challenge so we had to add a water line to the craft building.

The first day our girls were thrilled to see the sample basket and were told this would be their craft for the week. Here's what we heard from our campers: "I'm going to make that?!" and "I'm sure it won't turn out like hers!"

The first day was an easy project of weaving the base. The second day brought much frustration as they attempted to bend the spokes up and weave the first weaver. The clothespins were always in the way, and sometimes the girls missed a spoke and had to start all over again. Ugh! "This basket weaving is difficult." Some wanted to give up.

But on the second day, they were excited as the weavers began to pull the basket tight together. The girls had to do four weavers up, and then they could add the dyed colored weaver of pink, green, or purple. They left craft class on Tuesday feeling excited. On Friday they were pleased and excited to show their mothers. Comments like *"this is the best thing I have ever made"* was common.

We have done this basket-weaving project every other year for the past fifteen years, and it has been great. I have never been able to be the kind of art teacher that says, "Here are the materials. Now use your creative abilities and make something." It is not a talent or ability I have been given. I have always taught crafts believing that a camper could make something very nice just by following oral instruction; a step at a time, the entire class together, and using material that will give the craft value for years to come.

I discovered ministry could be taught while creating the baskets. As an example, all reed has a smooth and a rough side. We want the smooth side on the outside of the basket and the rough side on the inside. That is an example of each of us letting people see the good inside our hearts and not the bad attitudes we sometimes have.

Reed also has to be wet in order for it to be pliable and bend. If it isn't wet it will crack. We need to be pliable in our relationships with family and friends, and sometimes only God can work in our hearts to accept other people. Finally, baskets are made to hold things like bread. Jesus is called the Bread of Life, and do we hold Him in our hearts?

For the most part, fifth and sixth grade campers appear quiet, and we do not know what they are thinking (especially the boys). Ministry can take place in the hearts of these young people, even in crafts, though we may not be aware of it. A special sixth grade boy gave my husband, Jim, a hug before leaving crafts each day. He had a personality that melted everyone's heart, but his family situation was very difficult. This young man came to camp two weeks in a row, learned his memory work, climbed two sides of the tower, and sat at our lunch table to just talk. But on Friday, the last day, he looked like he was close to tears.

On Friday afternoon our staff lined up to be introduced at closing ceremonies and do our *high fives* as we pass by the campers. Jim was behind me as we ran through. As we turned to run back into the pavilion, the long line of staff behind me stopped. I looked back to see this young man get up from his seat on the floor and stop Jim to give him one more hug. He indeed so needed a loving father in his life. We pray that he will seek his heavenly Father and find the peace and the power of Jesus Christ, that he learned at camp, to continue through the difficult and lonely times of his young life.

TWENTY–SIX
Additional Program Facilities for Camp

WHEN WE ADDED additional weeks of summer camp and incorporated camps for our older youth, we found we had a crucial need for additional facilities. These new facilities helped us stretch out into undeveloped areas of the camp and allowed us to create programming that enhanced our themes. We were using all of the thirty-three acres Harv Chrouser instructed us to use.

ƺ ƺ ƺ ƺ ƺ ƺ ƺ

Sandlot Playground and Volleyball Court

In the late 1980's, when we began our winter activities of tubing and skiing we thought it would be a good idea to add a skating rink. We had a number of pairs of skates donated, and all we needed was a place to hold water to freeze for a rink. We asked a gentleman from our church if he was willing to bulldoze an area behind the Activity Center for the rink. Jim and I were out of town for the weekend when he arrived to do it.

When we came home on Sunday night, we were overwhelmed with the size of the hole. It was about *three times* the size we had expected. Oops! It measured eighteen inches deep and almost a half of an acre in size. Now what were we going to do with this large dug out area? Our attempts at a skating rink fell through year after year, so eventually we decided to fill the area with sand for a volleyball court and playground.

It ended up being a great asset to the ministry and in exactly the right place – the center of all activity. Again, God took our mistakes and created something that was a bonus to our ministry and a busy, safe place when small children are on the camp property.

ᴤ ᴤ ᴤ ᴤ ᴤ ᴤ ᴤ

Mini Golf Course – 1991

Early in our *Mountain Doo Dayz* theme (about 1987), we wanted to put in a Goofy Gopher Golf Course for one of the afternoon activities. I envisioned it back on the hilly part of the far lot that used to be pasture for our horses. Jim mowed nine putting greens in the back field. He buried soup cans for the holes, and my father made golf clubs out of yardsticks from NAIER. We used walnuts instead of golf balls. On the last hole, the campers had to hit the walnut through an irrigation pipe and follow it down into the hole. It was a great success. The campers had a ball! But it was a tedious job to keep the grass mowed all summer, and there was no shade in the field.

The next time *Mountain Doo Dayz* was a few months off, Jim said, "No back field mini-golf course this year." Again, I was set in my mind to have a Goofy Gopher Golf Course. It was such a neat idea, and it went well with the theme and was a blast for the campers. The walnuts didn't exactly go where the campers hit it, and the silly golf clubs went so well with the goofy *Mountain Doo Dayz* theme.

All winter I pleaded with Jim to build us a mini-golf course. But Jim said it would cost too much and be too much work.

Well, God knew the desire of my heart.

Jim was on the CCCA state board of directors, and he went to the monthly meeting at in Hillsdale, Michigan. When he came home that night, he said, "I got you a mini-golf course. Now all we have to do is haul it." Jim had mentioned to someone that we wanted a mini-golf course, and the director of the camp said he had one he would be willing to give away. He was thrilled to get rid of it. God did it again!

He supplied us with an eighteen-hole course. It only cost us the amount of the new green carpeting – what a deal!

Not long after that, a dentist in Bridgman built a new office on a plot of land that had a mini-golf course on it. He donated a large alligator, a tall pelican, and a cannon to add to our course. We were also given multiple golf clubs and God provided Five Pines with a great source for used golf balls. We knew we had been blessed. I was so excited because God *again* answered my prayers.

ᘓ ᘓ ᘓ ᘓ ᘓ ᘓ ᘓ

Archery Range – 1994

When we moved the day camp crafts over to the east side of the property, we decided to also clear land next to the Craft Cottage and add an archery course. We needed this kind of programming for our first through fourth grade campers. Eventually the archery program became so popular; we kept it on the schedule for the Adventure Campers who were in fifth and sixth grade. It is surprising to see something as simple as archery brings so much excitement and challenge to our young campers.

God supplied this program through the wonderful generosity of two different schools. One donated all their archery equipment from their physical education program. In 2009 we wanted to upgrade to compound bows for Adventure Camp, and students from another school raised the money for us to purchase the new bows. God continued to provide for our desires in a miraculous way.

TWENTY-SEVEN
The Completed Pattern

THE CHALLENGE we soon faced was how do additional programming and use our facilities year-round. At this time most camps only did programming during the summer months, but Jim had a vision to extend our programming for all twelve months. It would be easier to keep staff, create a consistent monthly income, and add additional promotional opportunities for our important summer camps.

If we did camp in the summer, hay rides in the fall, snow tubing and cross-country skiing in the winter, and another program during the spring and fall months, our calendar would be full. Many other camps were surprised that a small camp like Five Pines could generate year-round programs. Most camps didn't have any winterized buildings, and our well-insulated and heated Activity Center allowed us to host groups and do activities even in the winter. Jim had a vision for winter activities on a tubing hill, and God had plans for more.

𝟆 𝟆 𝟆 𝟆 𝟆 𝟆 𝟆

Tubing Hill – 1982

As long as we can remember, the hill out back has been a sliding hill. It used to be a peach orchard when Five Pines was a farm. Tanya and Kirk and neighborhood friends spent hours on their sleds and toboggans on a winter day zooming down the hill. At that time there were many more trees, and the hill wasn't as high or as deep at the bottom as it is now. I remember fighting the fear that my own children might suffer head injuries as they sped down the hill on their toboggan, narrowly escaping a collision between the two trees that they had to go between. The two trees stood right in the middle of the hill.

Jim thought that the hill could be made steeper with a little work. So in 1982, he began to clear a path much wider than what our children had – enough for two runs. Every time he excavated an area for a new project, he added the excess dirt to the top of the hill. Eventually he had to reinforce the top with railroad ties and build a set of steps to climb to the top.

I will never forget the winter Jim finished off the steps to the top of the hill. The reason I recall that experience is because it was freezing cold and sleeting. The last place I wanted to be was outside building a stairway to get to the top of the tubing hill. But we had scheduled our first group of the season for the *next day*, and the steps needed to be completed!

The winter programming has been most rewarding to us, as we witness the endless line of cars packed with little kids coming to Five Pines to enjoy the "Thrill of the Hill". What excitement in their little hearts to go so fast down that "Big" hill.

I love to watch the dads hauling their young children up the hill only to go down again and again. What a privilege to offer such a neat activity for families on the land God gave to Jim – and Jim gave back to God. Harv said use it all and Jim did.

One time back in the early days of the tubing hill, one of our board members, Dr. Richard Roach, wanted his daughter's birthday party out at Five Pines. Tirza invited about fifteen of her friends to come and tube. The temperature began to drop during the afternoon, and the sun shone continually as well. The kids had gone down the hill repeatedly, and what was once snow-packed was now very icy in the late afternoon. Those seven and eight- year-olds went whizzing down at a pretty good rate of speed! I knew the next day we had scheduled a group of special education students to tube, and I was worried.

But God did a miracle. The next day when the special education students came, the temperature had warmed up considerably. I'm sure Tirza's friends would have been bored with the slow hill, but for these special students the speed was perfect. Their reaction time was very slow, and it took them longer than other children to get off their tube at the bottom of the hill (to get out of the way of the next tube coming). They were safe, they had a great time, and the hill was perfect for them. God is so faithful. He cares about the little things like the condition of a tubing hill for these young special needs students.

Back in the early 1980's when Jim was still working for Whirlpool, he would let groups come out during the week and use the hill. One beautiful winter day a group of students came out from Hartford Federated Church. Tim was their youth pastor. We had built a good relationship with him through the Non-Proms, so we let his youth group enjoy the day out on the hill. They were the only group out there, and I was in the house.

Soon there was a knock on the door. It was two of the students, and they said someone was knocked out on the tubing hill! I immediately put on my coat and rushed out to the hill. I soon found out that it was their youth pastor. By the time I got out there, Pastor Tim had come to and was alright. It was such a scare to me, especially since Jim wasn't there. In the thirty-plus years we have had the tubing hill, there have been a few collisions. It happens mostly when people don't get off their tube at the bottom and the next one down the hill collides with them (or knocks their feet out from under them).

Jim soon felt it was important for the participant's safety to not allow anyone on the hill without a staff person on duty. This has helped prevent many accidents and regulate the hundreds of people on the hill on weekends. Otherwise people do whatever they want and do not always use their common sense or foresee danger in their actions. We have had groups build ramps or jumps on the hill when a staff person was not there. It may have been fun, but it is dangerous to little ones.

One Saturday afternoon, I noticed a father who was stacking *three* tubes on top of each other. Then he put his child on the top of the tubes to send him down the hill. Believe me; I could not get out there fast enough. Other people have tried to *ski* down the hill! One little guy ran ahead of his family and was so excited that he ran to the top of the hill and jumped down. He went down all the way on his bottom without a tube.

We eventually added lighting for night tubing, built a staff shelter at the top, enlarged the steps to double wide, molded the runs, and expanded the entire hill to five runs. We have seen *thousands* of people on the hill and an average of 250 to 300 people a day on the weekends.

In the beginning of our winter tubing program, Jim ordered a large supply of truck tubes. We soon discovered that the truck tubes had too large of a hole in the middle, and the little kids fell through! So he went to car tubes. Eventually we were using one hundred tubes a year, and even then Jim spent endless hours repairing them.

In 2004, Jim ordered a commercial grade of tubes that had a fiberglass bottom with canvas around the top to hold the tube in. They turned out to be *much* faster but *much* safer. It was an expensive proposition with the tubes costing $90 apiece, but Five Pines received a donation to cover the purchase. Five Pines is still using the same tubes ten years later with very little breakage of the inner tube. We have also added more tubes and even purchased a few double tubes (which work well for families with their toddlers).

The winter tubing has been a great activity for families. There were times when over one hundred people would be waiting to get on the hill and the return line would *begin* where the people got off their tubes at the bottom. Then there could be another seventy-five or eighty people inside the Activity Center eating pizza and hot dogs. Some weekends people would be standing wall to wall in the Activity Center to warm up with their hot chocolate before heading out to the hill again.

In the winter of 1998, we were expecting two hundred 4H members for a night of tubing. It was near the end of winter, and we were desperate to stretch the snow on the hill at least one more night. The top launching area was nearly bare. We decided to haul snow from hills around the parking lot, but it was icy snow and hard. So our creative program director solved the problem by putting the icy snow through a wood chipper! Soon we had a beautiful layer of crushed snow on the top of the hill, and the 4H kids had a wonderful time. The next day it all began to melt.

That story has been told over and over because of the inconsistency of our Michigan winters. One day we have snow and cold temperatures, and then the next day temperatures rise up into the 40's and everything melts – and a group is scheduled. Through it all, though, God has always supplied us with what we need.

♒ ♒ ♒ ♒ ♒ ♒ ♒

Purchase of a Snow Machine – 1999

In 1998, a generous supporter donated a Pontiac Grand Prix to Five Pines and it sold for $7,500. We used the money to obtain snowmaking equipment for the hill. In order to set up the snow maker, we needed a 10,000-gallon storage tank (donated by Andrews University in Berrien Springs), a portable air compressor that could maintain at least one hundred pounds of pressure, a motor, and a pump. Different people played an important role in getting us this equipment. Most of the equipment was donated, and some we had to purchase. We also had to construct a building to store the equipment.

In order to make snow, the temperatures have to drop to twenty-five degrees or below. Night after night the lights would go on, and Jim, Eric Sandberg, and other staff would spend the wee hours of the night making snow on the hill. The crew would work until they ran out of water, and then the tank would take another eight hours to refill before they could make snow again. This seemed like an impossible dream, but again God supplied all our needs. In the years to come, *thousands* of people have loved the "Thrill of the Hill". After the initial nights of making snow, God usually takes over and the hill is iced for the next two busy months.

ʚ ʚ ʚ ʚ ʚ ʚ ʚ

Cross Country Skiing – 1982

When our son, Kirk, was in high school, he was an intern at Sarett Nature Center in Benton Harbor. He taught himself how to ski and taught cross-country ski lessons during the year he was at Sarett. Kirk was eager to establish cross-country ski trails here, so he groomed many trails not only on our property but also on the 180 acres of land we were leasing next to Five Pines. He was excited about the winter sport and encouraged us to include cross-country skiing in our winter programming.

Kirk challenged Jim and me to learn to ski. The first year that I was on skis, I never got out of the front yard! Kirk had cut a practice loop for me. The next year, I attempted to go out on some trails and discovered it was almost more difficult to get back up in the deep snow after falling than it was to ski. Learning to get up became a great accomplishment for me. But it wasn't long before I fell in love with the challenge of cross-country skiing and eventually helped teach it to school groups at Five Pines.

Breaking a ski trail through eight inches of new-fallen snow is not easy, and I was the person to break the trails (before we owned a snowmobile). I have put more time than I really want to admit in breaking trails for our school groups or weekend guests. Jim found out that we could purchase a grooming sled that could be pulled behind a snowmobile and make a perfect trail in the snow. It cost about $300 and would last forever. It was worth it, and we still use it to groom those wonderful ski trails today.

We received a donation of two very large snowmobiles that were used to groom trails in Northern Michigan. One day Jim took one of the snowmobiles and left to groom the trails over on the 180 acres we were leasing. After many hours he finally came back – walking! The snow was very deep, and he had that huge monster of a snowmobile stuck. (This was before cell phones.) He was exhausted.

Eventually we received a smaller snowmobile, and that made

our job easier. Of course keeping a snowmobile running during crucial times has been an ongoing challenge. In the period of thirty years, we have gone through as many as ten used snowmobiles, and Jim's dear friend Earl has worked on all of them (not just once but many times).

One day God miraculously provided a snowmobile when ours was out of commission. Our program staff was near panic as the Niles school bus drove up and between fifty and sixty students got out. The students were spending the day at Five Pines to learn how to ski and have a blast on the tubing hill.

We had one very large problem.

We had experienced one of those lake effect snowstorms overnight, and about eight inches of heavy snow made the ski trails impassable. But before we were able to relate our problem to the teachers, someone drove up on a snowmobile and parked in front of the Activity Center. The lady on the snowmobile was an aunt to one of the students. She had heard that her nephew was coming to Five Pines, and she drove over from Eau Claire to see him.

We related the problem with our snowmobile and the deep snow and asked if she might be able to help groom the trails. Sure enough, she was willing to hook up to our groomer, take a staff person with her, and groom our trails! She was indeed an answer to prayer, and we hadn't even had time to pray! The day turned out to be absolutely beautiful, the trails were perfect, and all of the students had a great time. Thank You, Lord. These times are precious memories and another God-inspired thread in our Tapestry.

It wasn't long before cross-country skiing became a popular winter program drawing groups from all over Southwestern Michigan and Northern Indiana (as well as our weekday school groups). We were drawing mostly church youth groups and a little interest from the general public.

Love Creek Nature Center was located just north of us on Huckleberry Road. Two years after we began our ski program, Love Creek created ski trails and began a ski program open to the public. A year later, we received what was basically a "hate letter" from the person who was outfitting their program with skis. The letter said that Five Pines was stealing his income and had copied his program (even though we had begun cross-country two years *previous* to their initial ski program). He also said in the letter we were not Christians but of the devil. This was an angry man with much hate in his heart.

So we prayed about this accusation. We responded by saying that we would inform our guests that Love Creek also had ski trails and ski rental. We even included an ad on the back of our ski brochure that let people know about Love Creek's cross-country skiing.

In discussing this with the naturalist at Love Creek, we were informed that he was not aware of the letter and felt badly about it. He and his staff did not feel the same way as the outfitter and apologized for it. To this day both places have trails and equipment. Each has its own clientele: Love Creek has more difficult trails for more serious skiers, and ours are easier and for those who are starting to learn about cross-country skiing.

Because Five Pines was able to offer both the tubing hill and the cross-country skiing, we were able to draw schools during the week and families on the weekends. When we have had a winter of abundant snow, we could also offer our school groups igloo building and a winter survival class. There is no busier place when there is snow than Five Pines. The weekdays are usually booked with area school groups and often a night birthday party. So over the months of January and February, there have been years where we were almost non-stop with tubing and skiing groups. It takes a lot of prayer to keep us all going with few breaks.

꒰ ꒰ ꒰ ꒰ ꒰ ꒰ ꒰

Sugar Creek Ministries - An Example of God's Love

Groups from southern Indiana and Illinois would book a retreat at Five Pines because of the winter activities and because we were near a downhill skiing resort in Jones, Michigan. For about ten years, a group of students from various churches in Illinois called Sugar

Creek Ministries came north to South Bend for a weekend retreat. They would bring around one hundred students. On Saturday of their retreat, about half of the students would go downhill skiing in Jones, Michigan, and the other half would spend the day at Five Pines.

One Saturday when the Sugar Creek group was at Five Pines, I was able to witness one of the most heartwarming illustrations of God's love that I have ever experienced.

At first one father and his son just stayed in the Activity Center, while everyone else was on the hill or on the ski trails. I noticed that his son was a special needs child, and the father demonstrated a very warm expression of love in addressing his son. The two of them spent most of the afternoon inside. Later in the day, they came into the ski shop and asked about the trails and how to ski. They decided to try their hand at skiing.

I tried to simplify the idea of cross-country skiing and told them what trails to take that would be the least challenging. They were gone for quite a while, and I wondered how they were doing. I went out the ski room door and spotted them coming back. Tears welled up in my eyes and my heart broke.

For there on the return trail came the father on his skis, poles in hand – and his son on his back. The son's skis stuck out on both sides of his father, and his hands with the poles were wrapped around his dad's neck. They had only skied part of the one trail, and the young man had gotten tired.

That loving father carried his son all the way back, one small stride at a time. This picture will be imbedded in my mind forever. It so clearly exhibits what God does with us every day through His love and endurance. God carries us through all circumstances and with an even *greater* love than this very special father demonstrated with his very special son.

To this day, I look back and think about the challenge of learning to cross country ski. It certainly was one of the most difficult activities I ever had to master. I like to be in control, and I wasn't always in control of those skis! It has turned out to be one of the most enjoyable activities I have learned. I have had knee replacement surgery on both of my knees, and at one point I was scheduled for back surgery. But I can hardly wait to have the trails to the east of our house tracked so I can go out and ski. Late in life, I learned that if we only step out and try new things; we certainly can enhance the value of our lives.

ᕘ ᕘ ᕘ ᕘ ᕘ ᕘ ᕘ

Maple Glen Retreat Center

We had to make plans for additional restroom facilities in the late 1980's. Up until this time, the only public restrooms were the two small single stalls in the Activity Center. When we started our day camps in 1985, our campers had to change into their swimsuits in a pop-up camper in addition to the Activity Center restrooms. We also felt the need for a pavilion-type structure for inclimate weather. Jim also had plans to build a new swimming pool to meet state requirements, since we were using the small twenty-foot by forty-foot pool we had installed in 1972 for our own family.

So in 1988 we began a fundraising project entitled "Project Upgrade". Jim had a group on a Boundary Water Trip when the first donation came in: $5,000. I was so excited, but I had no one to share my excitement with because everyone on staff was out of town. When Jim came home, we shared our joy and gratitude with the couple who had so generously given to this project. This dedicated Christian couple had owned a grocery store in Niles and just sold it, sharing a portion of the sale with Five Pines. Our "Project Upgrade" fundraiser brought in $25,000 to help meet a goal to build a covered pavilion with restrooms.

During that summer, Bill Deetjen and his crew were hired to pour the cement floor. As he installed the floor, he poured four-foot footings all around the base. We questioned this, since it was only to be an outside pavilion. His comment to us was, *"Well someday you may want to build a two-story building on this."* We laughed, but it represented a thread in our Tapestry we hadn't planned on. Many years later a two-story dorm addition was added and the four-foot footings were important. Who would have thought – only God!

As the restrooms and small kitchen area were becoming a reality, we experienced another act of God. Our neighbor, who owned Eau Claire Lumber Company at the time, stopped by one day. He suggested, "Without too much effort and expense, you could turn this pavilion into a year-round facility by just enclosing the walls, insulating, and installing a furnace."

Jim had always desired to have a retreat center, but it was not in his plans now and not in this location. Obviously God had other plans. (Remember in 1979 when Dr. Bob Patton and Jim started praying and faithfully prayed for two years for a retreat facility? God began to answer those prayers after ten years of working with people!)

The wheels began to turn. Could this be worth a consideration? We added the enclosed pavilion and the thought of a possible retreat center to our prayer list. Walt Arney Construction Company had built the rafters to span across the width of the building, but we could easily build interior walls to separate the rooms.

As we began to research the possibility, the cost wasn't that much to enclose the exterior walls. We were given a reasonable price on blown insulation AND a new geothermal Water Furnace was offered free of charge by Michiana Water Furnace (owned by Mark Wurzel). Mark was one of our very first participants in our wilderness trips and *Fifth Quarter* programs. He too became a major supporter of the ministry and certainly a very brightly-woven thread on the Tapestry. Major supporters have been woven in and out of every project Five Pines has attempted. (We could not have done any project without large AND small gifts.) Mark is still extremely faithfully active today.

We divided the main room into three separate rooms. One was a small dining room closest to the kitchen, and the other two were dorms. Harv Chrouser arranged for us to receive a shipment of used wooden bunks from Honey Rock Camp and also dining room tables and chairs. Some dear friends purchased a salad bar for Five Pines at a community college auction. We began to look very professional in food service! We now had the restrooms we needed, plus a year-round facility for retreats and an additional building for day camp programming.

Over the years, this small retreat center was used by hundreds of groups. In 1990, twenty- seven different groups from Michigan, Indiana, and Illinois enjoyed the small facility known then as Maple Glen Retreat Center. Buses would drive up and unload the students. The youth pastor and adult sponsors were eager to implement the programs presenting the jewels of the Word of God to help their young people grow in Christ. The kitchen was fully-equipped with kitchen cabinets, appliances, and everything else needed to prepare meals. All of it was supplied by donations from various people. Our guest groups often shared with us how much they loved being at Five Pines. The comment so often was, "I can feel God here."

The building, however, was not able to accommodate many of the groups who were interested in having a retreat with us. The very small dining hall was inadequate as were the two dorm rooms. There was only a four-inch wall between the girls and boys dorm. Unknown to us, a small hole "developed" in the wall between the girls and the guys rooms. A peep hole so to speak. The youth pastor, whose young people "discovered" it, claimed it was there when they came. We knew this was not the fact, but it did add to our concerns that there was a definite need to enlarge and upgrade the retreat center.

In a letter to Jim's board members in 1999, he brought them up to date on our retreat schedule. He mentioned the following:

"We are currently getting ready for a retreat of eighty-one people. We have bunks up in every square inch we could find. Michiana Christian Service Camp loaned us enough beds to sleep everybody. We have converted both the "L" room and the ski room in the Activity Center, filled the Craft Cottage with bunks, plus the dorms in Maple Glen. I think we can get them all in now. They have agreed to eat in shifts. Boy that addition to Maple Glen would be nice!"

So our board approved a project to open up the dining hall of Maple Glen and add additional space with two-story dorm rooms as well as a lounge. We needed to enlarge the kitchen as well. It would be no easy project.

☙ ☙ ☙ ☙ ☙ ☙ ☙

Maple Glen Retreat Center Addition
The Carriage House Lodge - 2000

We obtained finances in 1997 through both a grant and a donation to seek the advice on a long-range site planner. Howard Deardorff was hired to help us plan our future. One of his recommendations was to build a two-story dorm addition to the present one-story Maple Glen. We remembered when Bill Deetjen poured four-foot footings for what was then a pavilion back in 1988. His prediction had come true. Jim began to draw up plans with an estimated cost of $100,000 for the addition.

Grants were written to various organizations. The Frederick S. Upton Foundation awarded Five Pines a challenge grant of $10,000 over a two-year period. We were able to match the Upton grant and raise enough additional funds to start the project.

Construction on the two-story 67,000 square-foot addition began on May 1, 2000. Included in this addition were a spacious lounge, a small storage room, and four dorms on the main level. On the lower level we added a small game area, a storage room, men's restroom, and four dorm rooms. The new addition would sleep thirty-two people on each level (eight to each dorm room) for a total of sixty-four participants. When you add the overflow bunks, we could accommodate up to eighty people.

We also expanded the kitchen with the addition of more donated cabinets, a large and deep double sink, and a commercial dishwasher. A large twelve-foot by seven-foot walk-in cooler/freezer was also installed. The boys had a new restroom on the lower level, so we remodeled the two side-by-side restrooms on the main level to become one large restroom for the girls. That provided four shower stalls for them.

By adding our Maple Glen Retreat Center and then enlarging it as the Carriage House Lodge, God allowed us to expand our outreach to many different organizations: universities, schools from Indiana and Illinois, and retreats for men and women. God blessed us with many falls and winters of a full schedule, and we had a steady stream of people coming to this little ministry back on an old gravel country road with orchards all around and called Five Pines.

ℨ ℨ ℨ ℨ ℨ ℨ ℨ

The Hand of God in Laying Floor Tiles

God miraculously directed our workers in the remodeling effort to open two restrooms into one. Many years before, a college student was home over Christmas break and asked if we had a job for him to do. The two restrooms only had painted cement floors, and we wanted tile installed. Mark had *never* laid tile before but was willing to give it a try. He proceeded to lay the tile in the girl's restroom. Then he proceeded to go around to the boy's restroom and laid the tile in that room. He never thought, nor did we ever plan, to combine the two restrooms into one.

But God knew.

When the wall that separated the girls and boys restrooms was taken out and the vinyl tile flooring was repaired, *the twelve-inch by twelve-inch tiles lined up perfectly!* With God all things are possible. We have witnessed the hand of God in so many events like this in our lives.

In 2001 a twelve-foot by thirty-four-foot storage room was built on the west end of the retreat center. The additional storage was required to store the twelve round tables and chairs for the dining room. We also needed more space for food storage. We remodeled the small room off the lounge, which was the original storage room, as an additional dorm room for a speaker or sponsors of our retreats.

The kitchen had to be licensed by the Michigan Department of Health if we were going to do food service for our guest groups. We also knew that if we licensed the kitchen, then we would have to limit its use to our staff only. Jody Fisher had been our fabulous summer cook during day camp but was not available to cook for our retreats. Five Pines would have to hire a cook, and I was adamant that the cook was *not* going to be me. It was a road I did not want to ever go down.

When all construction was completed on the lodge, we were excited to do a beautiful job of interior decorating. It was so much of the goods we received from NAIER such as: the heavy grade vinyl wallpaper, drapery fabric, dinner dishes, tablecloths, large kitchen cabinets, and some windows, almost at no cost. We eagerly made beautiful drapes for the dorm rooms and draw drapes for two large French doors in the lounge. It was exciting to see God at work.

In my heart I knew God was a great *exterior* decorator from all the beauty in nature, but He also proved to be an outstanding *interior* decorator. God's provision for this new lodge made the building a very attractive place inside. Our finished product was beautiful, and we still receive comments to this day about the "homey feel" people enjoy when they experience a retreat at Five Pines.

During this renovation of the retreat center, we changed the name from Maple Glen to the Carriage House Lodge. Our site planner, Howard Deardorff, had suggested we choose a theme décor for the buildings in our camp to bring unison to our grounds. Five Pines was not a backwoods rustic camp with log cabins. The original house gave more of a classic estate feeling, and therefore we needed to tie all of our buildings in with that idea in mind. So the retreat center became the lodge, and the exterior motif of the present and future buildings will continue with that estate décor. The Activity Center was the original barn and would stay that way – a barn on the estate.

ह ह ह ह ह ह ह

Carriage House Rafters Rebuilt – 2005

Although the rafters over the dining hall were built to span the entire width of the building and not need a supporting wall in the middle, they began to sag when the weight of snow built up. The new addition in 2000 was attached to the north side of the dining hall roof, and the weight of snow that built up where the two roofs came together was just too much. A few of the original rafters were cracked.

So in January of 2005, we had to tackle a major rebuild of the ceiling structure. There were a number of retreats scheduled in February, but the ceiling had to be fixed. We needed to tear the ceiling out and re-enforce the rafter structure which Walt Arney had constructed in 1988. This was a major job. Our maintenance staff was involved in construction for our new office, but the entire staff had to put their energies on the roof of the Carriage House.

In came the scaffolding, down came the drywall, and reconstruction began. But in just one month the job was completed. Praise the Lord for the gracious help from those dear old friends who are always there when we need help and a hard-working staff. The problem was finally solved.

ཟ ཟ ཟ ཟ ཟ ཟ ཟ

Food Service for Carriage House Lodge

"Give me, Lord, what You command, and command what You desire." Augustine

In 2002, I took the big step of Guest Group Coordinator and Food Service Director. That year the Carriage House Lodge was booked every weekend through April 15. Full food service was initiated for all guest groups.

My mother was an excellent cook. She could always cook better than anyone else, therefore I had many fears of failing in the kitchen. She always said she didn't want a mess, and she would rather do it herself. When Jim asked me to marry him, I responded, "I don't even know how to cook!" I have never felt a joy of cooking – especially for other people. I hated to go to potluck dinners for fear my dish would never get eaten. I remember standing in the doorway of the Carriage House kitchen watching Jodi Fisher prepare meals for campers and counselors. I would say, "Jodi, I just don't know how you do it. I could *never* cook for a large group of people!"

After saying "no" for two years and not finding anyone else, I went fighting and kicking and ventured into the kitchen of the Carriage House Lodge. I felt that it was not my expertise, but God would have to equip me. I still feel much anxiety today when I think of what I was asked to do. But despite my fears and feeling of inadequacies, I was able to do the cooking. With God all things are possible, and God can equip us with abilities we don't think we have.

I treasure a quote from Chuck Swindoll: *"You have to let your capacity be invaded by God's power."* This looked like an impossible thing for me. But remember God had led me through many things that I thought were impossible. In the end, I was always a new person achieving heights I never dreamed of – and surprisingly enjoying them!

The challenges in my new position as "chief cook and bottle washer" were usually as many as six meals a weekend. Our retreats were for youth, college age, families, and just ladies or just men. When your cooking for such a variety of people, you can't always have the same menu. You do not want to serve hot dogs to a ladies retreat, but fifth and sixth graders are joyous and eat two or three of them. On the other hand, serving wonderful homemade soups, salads, and homemade bread to the ladies for lunch is not something junior high students enjoy (or appreciate!).

Regarding desserts, we found that a simple brownie with ice cream and lots of chocolate sauce brought "oohs and ahs" from almost *any* group. How simple, low in cost, and minimal preparation. We decided everyone was a chocolate lover, and no one turned down ice cream! Jim loved to carry the trays out. They all loved him and he loved doing it.

At times I didn't do all the cooking by myself. There were people who helped with recipes and ideas. Lisa had a wonderful Amish peach cobbler recipe, and Jodi left us with a very detailed cookbook which was worth its weight in gold. Different people would come in and help with some baking prior to the retreats. Basically it was a week-long process of buying and preparation.

Some college-age retreats could include four or five vegetarians, two vegans (no dairy), students with allergies, and students needing gluten-free meals. Oh my! Many challenges seemed to come with each and every group.

Way back in October 2002, we had nine overnight retreat groups scheduled *plus* three one-day groups participating in a challenge program. They all required food service (approximately 425 people). Along with this busy schedule, we did over 135 wagons for the hayride program. It wasn't easy juggling hosting guest groups, food service for those guests, and hay rides all at once. Praise the Lord we had a great staff.

Every year we hosted a ladies retreat from nearby Andrews University. Some ladies were just vegetarians and half of them were vegans. I confess that I learned how to make a "mean" carrot cake without any eggs or butter. Praise the Lord for *Google*. You can find a recipe for anything – even vegan lasagna.

What a blessing these ladies were. They loved Jim and me and showered us with gifts and flowers at each retreat. The leader knew what a challenge the food service was for them, and she was so appreciative. We began serving them in 2007, and they still come to Five Pines every year. In fact, if I look at the schedule of retreats today, we still serve the same ones from Illinois, Notre Dame, and Andrews University.

Each morning when we had to cook, Jim and I would get up at 6:00 a.m. and begin breakfast. Jim would flip those wonderful pancakes, and I would work on the scrambled eggs, fresh fruit, and coffee cakes. Jim's pancakes became the most popular item. Once during a men's retreat, they asked if the person who did the pancakes would come out and take a bow. Jim did and received an energetic round of applause. Then they asked if he would be willing to join them on a deer hunting trip and do all the cooking for them. *Little did they know that he did not know how to cook anything except pancakes and possibly French toast!* Obviously he bowed out of the deer hunting offer.

Every other year, we would host a retreat group of students

from Joliet, Illinois. They were from a variety of area universities. They came for a retreat of team building and informational classes about their spring mission trip to Bolivia. Natalie was a gracious older lady who was their leader and a dedicated person to the ministry in Bolivia.

Natalie was very sweet and very grateful to Five Pines and our staff (who did the team building portion of their retreat). In 2006, as Natalie and the group prepared to board their bus, she came over and said, "Your names will be on the altar in Bolivia for helping us bring our mission ministry group together. We will be praying for you." What a thoughtful blessing. My heart was so blessed.

Food service was the most difficult job I have ever done and yet the most rewarding. People like Natalie and the ladies from Andrews University made our day. Thank you, Lord, for giving us the opportunity to serve these people as they prepared to step out and serve people oceans away in Your name. We thank you, Lord, for allowing us to share our ministry, our hearts, and our faith with such wonderful, grateful people.

For those ten years I only did the cooking for retreats. We hired other ladies to do the cooking for the summer schedules.

When the pain in my back got so bad that I could not spend the long hours on that cement floor, I knew I had to step down. I panic every time I think about the years in food service. I'm not sure I could ever do it again. I am at ease and grateful to be out of it. But God was so very faithful to enable us to go way out of our comfort zone, accomplish things in His name, and meet some awesome people of God.

TWENTY – EIGHT
Threads of Continued Progress
"What is man that you are mindful of him, the son of man that you care for him?" – Psalm 8:4

BACK IN THE EARLY 1980's, when Jim first opened up the land and facilities to the public, he was asked if a group could bring out a number of children from Benton Harbor to swim in the pool. At the time, the only pool we only had was our small personal pool. The shallow end was not very long because it was a diving pool at the other end.

When the children arrived, there were *way* more than we had expected. No one listened to Jim's instructions. *They all just jumped in, and most of them who said they could swim … couldn't!* Chaos broke loose. Sharon Fedoruk was the lifeguard and there were a number of adults present as well. Suddenly everyone found themselves literally pulling the kids out one at a time. The one in front of me was going down for the second time, the one to my right was holding onto the edge for dear life, and it was a nightmare to say the least. Praise the Lord for being able to get them all out safely.

When we did those few years of inner-city camps, ninety percent of the campers did not know how to swim. Most of them had *never* been to Lake Michigan, even though they lived in Benton Harbor and very close to the lake. One important lesson we learned early on is to never trust children when they say they can swim. From then on it has been a priority to have a swim test and a session of swimming instruction each day of camp – no matter what the age. Most other camps do not offer swimming instruction but just a swim test. But we felt the value of swimming lessons for our campers at Five Pines. We do not certify our campers at any specific level, but instruction of some kind has been a must.

With the episode of our inner-city non-swimmers in mind, Jim made plans for a new larger commercial pool. It took a few years to acquire the funding for a new pool and, in the meantime, the old pool was used by our campers.

In 1991 we began a fundraising project, *"Pool Your Change to Change our Pool"*. By 1992 we had raised $31,226 for our new pool, plans were drawn up, and excavation of the site began. We envisioned a thirty-foot by sixty-foot shallow pool without the depth for diving. This would be a major building project.

Jim chose to have the pool installed to the west of the Activity Center. There was a small knoll there and excavating would be a major portion of the project expense. There was a large amount of dirt to get rid of. Rather than dig out the walls of the old pool by our house, we decided to fill it in with the dirt that was excavated for the new pool. We then landscaped the old pool hole by planting five Blue Spruce trees and an assortment of shrubs. We completed this newly-landscaped area with a ten-foot cross. Jim also decided to use a large amount of the dirt excavated to build up the top of the tubing hill.

The new pool was supposed to be ready for camp by the second week of June in 1993. But there were problems with the cement around the edge of the pool, and Bill Deetjen and his crew were not available to pour the cement until the very last weekend before camp started.

On Monday of camp week, we were still pulling up the excess cement that had fallen into the water (when the cement was troweled) and settled at the bottom of the pool. Tanya and her husband, Jerry, spent three days removing large pieces of concrete from the bottom of the pool. By Wednesday of that first week, our first campers were enjoying the wonderful new pool. The showers and restrooms were not completed until the following year, and our campers had to use the restrooms in the Carriage House Lodge to change.

A few years before we built the pool house, someone asked us if we had any use for three very large solar panels. With a new pool in mind and knowing it would help heat a very large pool, we told them "yes". They were stored in the maintenance building for a couple of years and then installed on the south roof of the pool house. They are still helping to warm the pool water with solar heat. God looked out for us, and His blessings exceed our small minds. Life is full of the little blessing as well as the large ones. God so often took care of us years in advance for what we would need.

The original pool house restrooms were built in 1994, with the help of a group of volunteers from Berrien Center Bible Church. What a blessing they were, and in no time the building was up and ready for summer camp. As our summer day camp enrollment increased, we needed more room. About five years later, our maintenance staff doubled the dressing room capacity by adding on to the west end of the buildings.

§ § § § § § §

Parking Lots – 1992

With the addition of the new pool and the Carriage House Lodge, we needed adequate parking for our guests. Kalin Construction Company so willingly provided Five Pines with huge truck loads of gravel and the machinery to spread it on the front parking lot. A wonderful donor was aware of our need for a back parking lot. He knew a trucker who hauled huge loads of dried corn to Chicago and was willing to bring Five Pines two full truck loads of gravel for the back parking lot.

The expense to Five Pines for both of these parking lot projects was zero because of generous people who lovingly gave and gave and gave to make this ministry what it is today. How wonderful! Once you see the woven threads of a gracious God in your life, it becomes a natural sense to see God in it all!

"Unbelief is actually perverted faith, for it puts its trust, not in a living God, but in dying men." A.W. Tozer

ㅇㅇㅇㅇㅇㅇㅇ

An Outdoor Pavilion (Finally) – 1997

In 1997, after receiving a $5,000 grant from the Upton Foundation, we constructed a large and much-needed outdoor pavilion in the wooded area just west of Maple Glen Lodge (as it was known at that time). When we went to order the rafters for the pavilion, we laid out our plans for the size. The gentlemen at the company said they had a set of rafters that someone had ordered and didn't take. He offered us a great price if we could adapt the size to our pavilion plans. The offer was certainly a gift with minimal cost involved. One man's mistake became a huge blessing to Five Pines. Our pavilion is a perfect size and the price was right.

ㅇㅇㅇㅇㅇㅇㅇ

Gast Memorial Basketball Court – 2001

Five Pines has been the recipient of many generous gifts from friends who care about young people. They want youth to be connected with a ministry where a relationship with Jesus Christ is important – and a place where they feel welcome.

The thought of having a nice basketball court was indeed a dream. Financially it seemed impossible. The land where we had pictured the basketball court was low, and it would require volumes of fill to level it out. But how were we going to get a basketball court and the finances to fill the lowland?

Don Gast's parents, Edward and Oral Gast, both played basketball many, many years ago when they were students at Baroda High School. They were known to be rather outstanding players in their own right. The Gast family decided to financially invest in a basketball court at Five Pines in their honor. We were so grateful for the involvement of all the siblings to help make this dream come true. The result of this wonderful family effort has been a beautiful full-size court with six baskets.

Often after school, either boys on bicycles or a carload of young men drive up to the basketball court and play and play – sometimes until dark sets in. How valuable to offer an escape from social media, and involvement in an activity which offers great exercise and competitive play. It is priceless!

ଥ ଥ ଥ ଥ ଥ ଥ ଥ

The Preserve

The 180-acre farm to the west of Five Pines consisted of some older apple orchards, a few open fields, and lots of wooded land. So in the beginning of Five Pines, Jim asked the owner if he would be willing to lease the seldom-used land to Five Pines for hayrides and cross-country skiing. He agreed to a very reasonable fee. So for years our autumn hayride groups enjoyed those beautiful two miles of trails with numerous hills, wooded land, and peaceful meadows. It was indeed a beautiful landscape for hayride trails.

While Kirk was still living at home, he created additional ski trails. Some were labeled "advanced", but they became a challenge to not just the advanced skier but anyone who ventured out on "Hot Chocolate Run" (the far west trails on our leased property).

We were also able to have access to the stream which meandered through the leased property. Early in our *Gold Rush Days* camp programming, we would use the creek area below the bluff to pan for gold. Our young prospectors would ride the covered wagon to the back country, pan for gold, and ride the covered wagon back to Five Pines. The solitude of being back in the woods created an absolutely perfect experience.

ജ ജ ജ ജ ജ ജ ജ

The Preserve Sold – Death of a Vision

But, when the "For Sale" signs started going up in 2000 on the farm land, our hearts sank. Lots on the property to the west of Five Pines were for sale, and a new subdivision called "The Preserve" was mapped out. We felt a deep loss of a very important aspect of our programming. Job's words expressed the feelings we were experiencing: *"The Lord gave and the Lord has taken away"* (Job 1:20). We could certainly relate to Job with the same emptiness.

The price of the lots seemed rather high by our standards, and we were hoping they wouldn't sell. But in only a few years those prime wooded lots on 180 acres were sold, and absolutely beautiful homes were being built. "The Preserve" became a popular place to live, and eventually all of the lots were sold.

Our hearts became very heavy as we prayed for God's guidance. God would have to present us with a "Plan B" for our hayrides, our cross-country skiing, and our place to pan for gold. Here is what our "B Plan" became:

- Our 45-minute hayrides were now shortened to about thirty minutes. The thirty acres of Five Pines land offered fewer areas to lengthen the trail. A thirty-minute ride was acceptable to our groups, and God did provide.
- The original farm land of Five Pines offered mostly flat land, small hills, and numerous wooded areas for ski trails. We could track three different trails offering different terrain to our skiers but not long-distance trails. As we evaluated our clientele, we realized that they were mostly families with little children or school groups on the average of fifth and sixth grade students. . Again God worked it out for us to see our purpose: our ministry to families and school children.
- Losing the creek shore and the wonderful wooded area to pan for gold seemed like a disaster. How could it be *Gold Rush Days*

and not have a place to pan for gold? The stream at the bottom of the hill was such a perfect place. Our experiences in Nome, Alaska where our son Kirk and his family lived for eight years, gave us the idea that we might be able to build a sluice for the panning of gold. Then God answered our prayers. The source of water for the snow machine in the winter could be used as a source for the sluice. Jim built the wooden sluice and trays with screen bottoms to wash and shake the sand out and then let the campers pick out their gold nuggets. God provided once again.

We also needed a story of how we obtained the gold, seeing that we really didn't now have a source. Thus became the story of Zeke and the thousands of gold nuggets that were found and stored in buckets of sand. Our young prospectors would proceed to wash the sand from Zeke's gold through the sluice at Five Pines. Real or not, our sluice worked out great. Our young prospectors had a great time, and the experience is worth a million gold-painted rocks.

In chapter five, Job's words reflect his belief in God and God's provisions: *"He performs wonders that cannot be fathomed, miracles that cannot be counted. He bestows rain on the earth; he sends water upon the countryside."* He also provides in countless ways for the tiny little camp ministry called Five Pines.

TWENTY–NINE

In Search of a REAL Office

WHEN WE COMPLETED our present Administration Building in 2006, no one could fully comprehend the journey we had taken from our first "office". This new Administration Building was indeed an impossible dream come true. It was like a castle to us with room to spare, and we moved in with no debt. We raised the full amount to build the office. The following is a history of all the places we called an office:

꒳ ꒳ ꒳ ꒳ ꒳ ꒳ ꒳

The Box Stall – 1983

In 1983, Jim's office consisted of a lone desk in what was once the box stall of the old barn. This small room had a cement floor and was also the "Ski Shop" for cross country skiing, with about ten sets of skis hung on the wall. It was also the kitchen with an old double-bowl stainless sink set into a plywood countertop which was propped up with two-foot by four-foot boards. Hot chocolate was provided for skiers, and we added a small refrigerator which contained soda pop.

In 1987, after we completed the main part of the Activity Center, Jim added two rooms to the north side. One was an L-shaped room for the ski room, and one was on the east end for the new wood burning furnace. We were left with an open section in between with a large window in the center to look out of. These additions on the back side of the Activity Center allowed us to move all the skis out of the office/kitchen/ski room, and Jim could add a bigger desk to his "small office".

ፘ ፘ ፘ ፘ ፘ ፘ ፘ

First Real Office – 1989

In six years, business picked up and we needed a real office! We actually needed space for *three* desks. I had begun to work on staff, and Nancy Poling served as a volunteer in the youth ministry position. We easily solved this by enclosing the section between the new ski room and the furnace room. Wow! We had an actual office with three desks and sliding glass doors to look out.

Our next BIG step was to get a COMPUTER. We were just moving into the 20TH century. I learned from Don Gast at Southwestern Medical Clinic that you can stick a small desk and a computer in any closet and call it an office. So we built a small closet into the furnace room, and we then had our own computer office.

Nancy knew how to use a computer, so we felt we were really in business in our new office: three desks, a computer, and three people on staff. We were moving up in the world of running a real ministry.

Jim's mother, Julia Scofield, had been living in the mobile home behind our home, but we moved her to a nursing home in 1990 when her health declined. It was very evident that Julia would not be returning to her mobile home, so we discussed the possibility of having the mobile home as our office. Julia did pass away in 1993.

If we moved out of the Activity Center office, we could open up the back wall of the Activity Center and create a lounge or "Sofa Room" (as it is known today). This would provide seating room for our guests during tubing and skiing season and a young people hang-out for our teen ministries.

ፘ ፘ ፘ ፘ ፘ ፘ ፘ

Mobile Home Office – 1991

Jim felt the mobile home would be a great office for our

growing ministry. Jim Wing had joined Five Pines in 1991 as Youth Ministry Director, and we were in need of actual office space. We did some remodeling as we moved into the mobile home. Jim Scofield had an office in what was the kitchen, Judy had an office in one of the bedrooms, and Jim Wing took over the back room. Mike Emerson was hired in 1993 as full-time office manager, and he took over the main office in what was once the living room. We had additional computers as well.

As time went on, we added more program staff and a maintenance man. In 2001, we had ten full and part-time staff, and it was wonderful! Five Pines' reputation for all programs became very well known. God was using some very godly people to share His love with not only young people but adults as well. Our staff was growing out of the mobile home office, though, so we moved some of our program staff to the small room west of the stage in the Activity Center.

Program people are program people, and they had their own "space" to create – and create they did. These were some of the best years of our ministry. We prayed together every morning, and a lot was added to the ministry. Creative juices flowed and we grew in so many ways. It was so rewarding and so much fun.

But the mobile home was drafty, falling apart, and we eventually needed a building where our staff was together. We also needed a building that was attractive to the public. So Jim began to draw up plans to build an administration building. He knew what the ministry needed and had a good eye in drawing the layout. It looked huge by all standards of our previous offices.

Once again, it would take the generosity of our donors and the hand of God to accomplish the project. Jim and I were very excited. We would have a place to store all of our props for camp, a place for our large program staff, and a nice office for Jim as director.

222

ॐ ॐ ॐ ॐ ॐ ॐ ॐ

Groundbreaking for a New Administration Building – 2004

We praised the Lord for progress toward our first goal of $75,000. When we reached that amount, the board of directors gave Jim permission to break ground!!! Jim's vision that began a long time ago was about to become reality.

The new two-level Administration Building was completed in 2006. Jim's original plan of five main offices, a foyer, and a large office for our program staff was perfect. The plans also included a full lower level board room and storage rooms. The total cost of the new office was just over $100,000 and was paid in full by its completion. Much of the work was done by Jim, board members, staff, and maintenance director Dave Heiniger. For the heating and air conditioning, Five Pines was again blessed with another Water Furnace from Mark Wurzel. God certainly used his people to fulfill Jim's dreams and those of our staff. They were coming true!

The Lord continued to amaze us as He provided the six office rooms with desks, office chairs, bookcases, and filing cabinets. A medical office was redecorating, and all the used office equipment (including a large table for board meetings plus chairs) was available to us. All we had to do is get a large box truck and go to a specific warehouse in South Bend, Indiana. Wow! What a gift from the Lord.

For years we had been keeping the thought of a new office in our minds. Whenever we went to NAEIR, we hoped to bring home items we felt would be needed in a new office building. Once we brought home an entire set of new kitchen cabinets (including the countertop) to equip a full kitchen for our staff. We also had been storing up commercial grade vinyl wallpaper, beautiful stained wooden blinds for all the windows, curtain fabric, and a beautiful chandelier for the front foyer. All of this was at no cost or practically no cost.

In fact, some years before building the new Administration Building, Jim had ordered from NAEIR a full pallet of rolls of the commercial wallpaper. I wasn't aware that Jim had ordered an entire pallet, so we didn't know what to do with it when it arrived. There was the entire pallet, loaded with wallpaper, sitting out in the driveway of our house. So we took one roll at a time into the house and stored them under all the beds upstairs. It was great having so much to work with, and it didn't cost us a dime! God was certainly in the miracle of our beautiful Administration Building.

There has always been a sad note in my heart about all the time and energies Jim invested into this new building. For in just a few months time, Jim retired from the executive director position. He hoped to stay on staff in a maintenance position, but that didn't materialize. He never was able to enjoy the office he had put his heart and soul into:

> *"Lord I am willing to ... Receive what you give*
> *Relinquish what you take, Lack what you withhold*
> *Suffer what you inflict, Be what you require"*
> Author Unknown

> *"What is peculiar to the good man is to be pleased and content with what happens and with the thread which is spun for him."* – Marcus Aurelius

Jim, a gentle God-fearing man, accepted all these things because it was his choice to move on and retire from the executive director position.

THIRTY

Long-Time Volunteers and Staff

THE THIRTY-FIVE YEARS of Five Pines Ministries would not have been possible without the staff and volunteers God brought into our lives. Their hearts were dedicated to the ministry of Christian camping and sharing Jesus with our community. Many of them brought into the ministry the expertise we didn't have.

Jim and Jane Markle and Sharon Fedoruk were with us from the very first day of day camp and are still involved as volunteer staff in the Kinder Kamp program each summer. Alice Maysick was my right-hand craft helper for over twenty-five years and a prayer warrior for the ministry.

Claire Benson, who just went home to be with the Lord, was indeed a faithful servant. Every spring, we'd find him riding on his little blue tractor applying weed spray on about ten acres of our lawn. For many years, he was also faithful to mow the large fields on a weekly basis. Along with his lawn care came his "heart care". He always asked us how things were going. We knew that he had a heart for the ministry and children as well as a desire to take care of the lawns.

Leo Smith, Larry Holben and Bill Wurzel spent hours of volunteer time on projects that would have otherwise cost us much money to have done. They are very talented, willing people who were ready anytime.

We have had a variety of maintenance directors who always had an endless list of projects to get done: Mark Dine, Eric Sandberg, Glen Stewart, Arron Bauer, Art Zimmer, and Dave Heiniger are but a few of the talented men who have kept the camp in good condition and were ready to build anything I asked of them.

Program directors or associates were hired to cover everything from day camp and Adventure Xperience with school groups (on the ropes course, climbing tower, or team building) to winter programming like tubing and cross-country skiing. Nancy Poling was our first in 1988, and then Tim Chaddok, followed by Jim Wing, Carter Newell, Anna Carpenter, Eric Sandberg, Greg Wright, Jon Ackerman, Sara (Eskew) Bauer, Ryan Elmer, Matt Poorman, Sara Klosterman, Tim Zebell, and Justin and Megan Rhode.

The need for more office staff grew with the increase of programming as Jeanne Wing, Leah Poorman, and Debbie Napp stepped in. Mike Emerson, has been an extremely valuable office manager since 1993 – almost twenty-five years. Five Pines has had the privilege to have some absolutely marvelous summer staff to help with camp in the roles of Bible teacher: Angela Strzyzykowski, Kristen Slattery, Jacob Quick, Jake Osborn, Holly Jacobs and Peter Anderson to name only a few.

Over the years we have had many wonderful aquatics directors, including Sharon Fedoruk and our daughter, Tanya. Summer after summer they would return in the dual role of lifeguard and swim instructor for the pool. Jess Hanson has been so faithful to fill that role recently for many summers. It seems like forever. Bless her heart.

ଯ ଯ ଯ ଯ ଯ ଯ ଯ

Earl the Pearl

God's Word speaks of the value of fine pearls. Many times God brings people into your lives who you value as much as a fine pearl. There are some people who just keep giving of themselves and offering their services at no cost.

One of our most valuable and faithful people God brought to Jim and this ministry is Earl Maxwell ("Earl the Pearl"). Earl has been Jim's right-hand man and has gotten him out of all kinds of fixes! It didn't matter whether it was automotive, lawn mower, snowmobile, snowplow, snow-maker, pickup truck, air compressor, or pulling Jim out of ditches. The first person Jim called was Earl whenever something mechanical went wrong. He would have what we needed or he could fix it.

Now granted it may not be on the day you expect or fixed the way you expected. (Wire and duct tape work on just about anything!) Sooner or later "Earl the Pearl" would show up in his three-quarter ton pickup wrecker, called "Ole Yeller", and fix it. Ole Yeller has since run out of steam, and Earl has had one truck after another. He has never ceased to show up, though, in time of need. Earl was and still is a pearl of untold value!

THIRTY–ONE

Encouragement and Support for Thirty-Five Years

"We always thank God, the Father of our Lord Jesus Christ, when we pray for you, because we have heard of your faith in Christ Jesus and the love you have for all the saints." – Colossians 1:3

IN THE EARLY YEARS OF FIVE PINES, when Jim and I first left our jobs and began full-time in the ministry, my father often expressed his fears that we were not going to make it. How would we survive? Raising support was a totally new concept to my parents. Their five dollar bill into the collection plate each Sunday was for the pastor and the maintenance of their church. Why would anyone give money to someone who is going to have a camp for kids? They continued to worry day after day. How were we going to make it?

But he did not know the Lord or the people of God. Daddy did not understand that His servants had a desire in their hearts to share the Gospel in *America* as well as around the world. My parents only knew of missionaries in other countries (and never personally). Through it all we knew that God would provide.

Jim desired that, with God's help, we could go on a partial missionary support so as not to drain the ministry for our income. We prayed for believers who were willing to sign on to help us with our missionary support income. God blessed us with a wonderful group of faithful people. Our home church, Berrien Center Bible Church, has supported us as missionaries almost from the beginning. For over thirty-five years, many of these gracious people have faithfully and lovingly continued to support us year after year (even when Jim retired in 2006 from the full-time director's position).

Dad and Mom were amazed as they witnessed the walk of these believers and their generosity out of the goodness of their hearts. *Their hearts began to understand.* More than once my father would express, with tears in his eyes, that he was totally amazed at the generosity of people who loved the Lord. Dad could not fathom when I showed him a check for a large amount designated for a project or program. Mom and Dad's eyes were opening to the goodness of God and His people.

As my parents moved closer to us and eventually in our home, we constantly shared what seemed like miracle after miracle that God was doing in our lives and in the ministry. All of this began a turning in their hearts and an accepting of Christ as their Savior. Mom would say, "These are *really* Christians."

Before their deaths in 2006, God spoke to each of their hearts with a love they had not known or previously understood. That love became very real in each of their lives. God's goodness overcame the darkness and they believed. My mother's favorite song was "How Great Thou Art" and it is etched on her tombstone. When I think of my parents, I think of this verse found in Job 42:5: *"My ears had heard of you but now my eyes have seen you."* For almost 90 years of their lives God was a vague part of their lives, they knew about him but didn't really understand God's grace through Jesus Christ. God removed those blinders and overwhelmed each of them with His love.

ℒ ℒ ℒ ℒ ℒ ℒ ℒ

Five Pines Goes International

"All over the world this Gospel is bearing fruit and growing, just as it has been doing among you since the day you heard it and understood God's grace in all its truth." – Colossians 1:6

In the very beginning of our walk with the Lord, when Tanya experienced her mission trip to Haiti, we desired to be in missions someplace in the world. Of course it didn't work out to serve the Lord in a foreign country. That wasn't where God wanted us. He kept us here in Berrien Center on a farm called Five Pines, in a house with five white pine trees in the front yard.

Instead of Jim and Judy going to all parts of the world, He has been spreading the Gospel all over the world with young people who were involved at Five Pines. They came to camp and served as SONIC counselors or staff in one or more of our programs. God tugged at their hearts to make known the Gospel wherever He sent them.

There are many former staff people in the far corners of the world, not just on short-term projects. They are on long-term mission assignments, doing the work of Jesus as proclaimed in the Great Commission in Matthew 28:19. It is such an honor to see their mission work being done in places like India, Thailand, Ukraine, and the Dominican Republic. They are teachers, youth leaders, pastors, nurses, or opening coffee houses – all with the desire of sharing Jesus with those the Lord directs into their lives. In the past, we have also had young people involved in missionary work in Africa and places in Asia we can't specifically mention. To know and follow these young people as they walk with the Lord is so exciting.

In John 12:24, Jesus tells his disciples as He predicts his death that *"unless a kernel of wheat falls to the ground and dies, it remains only a single seed. But if it dies, it produces many seeds."*

Harv Chrouser and Don Gast planted those seeds in Jim and I and then encouraged us to plant in others. These followers of Christ are now planting seeds all over the world. We pray for the safety of these faithful ones and a bountiful harvest for the Lord in the end.

"The man who loves his life will lose it, while the man who hates his life in this world will keep it for eternal life. Whoever serves me must follow me; and where I am, my servant also will be. My father will honor the one who serves me." – John 12:25

𒀖 𒀖 𒀖 𒀖 𒀖 𒀖 𒀖

A Major Thread: Releasing My Fears to God

WHEN GOD PLANTED A VISION in Jim's heart regarding Five Pines, I wondered how I would ever fit into those plans. I could never have dreamed way back in 1979 when Five Pines Ministries became incorporated that in the years that followed:

I, who couldn't swim and was terrified of water, would one day canoe through the Everglades and out into coastal ocean waters with five canoes filled with twelve teenagers...

I, who had not previously even slept in a tent, would hike thirty-five miles with a backpack on my back (multiple times). I would help Jim lead a group of teens through the Smoky Mountains, once coming out in two feet of snow...

I, who would have considered myself an introvert, would one day be Guest Group Coordinator and eagerly greet guests groups (many from universities), and openly and boldly share our testimony and the testimony of Five Pines with every group. (Previously I was so inhibited by people that I would stand at the kitchen window and refuse to go out and greet a guest group that had just arrived at Five Pines.)

I, who had never been to summer camp as a child and had absolutely no idea what went on at a youth camp, would one day be used by God to create a successful summer camp program for Five Pines Ministries and even teach seminars on day camp programming to other Christian camp leaders...

I, who was very adamant about never cooking meals for large groups, would one day find me, cooking six or seven meals every weekend for thirty-five people or more. A few of those years it was twelve weekends in a row for overnight retreat guests in our Carriage House Lodge. Even meeting the challenge of serving totally vegan and vegetarian menus for a three-day ladies retreat, year after year...

I, who would have thought that I was afraid of heights and thought that no one would climb the original 28-foot climbing tower, would one day climb forty feet on the new Goliath...

Never underestimate the power of the Lord in your life. John Piper says, *"Christian living is supernatural or it is nothing."* When one is sold out to Christ, your self-identity will radically be changed because you have a new Master. He will provide everything you need to accomplish His plan for your life. Again, I quote one of my favorite passages of Scripture:

"But the people who do know their God shall be strong, and do exploits." – Daniel 11:32b KJV

THIRTY – TWO

The Tapestry's Final Threads

"I am come that they might have life, and that they might have it more abundantly."
– John 10:10b KJV

I FELT LED TO WRITE THE TAPESTRY as a memoir of the life Jim and I have so humbly been privileged to live. We do not take lightly how God has led in the ministry. He is indeed an amazing God. We have grown in our faith, grown in our abilities, and grown in our boldness to share His love with others. Jim and I have grown closer to each other, more than we could ever imagine.

We have been privileged to walk through doorways that were opened to us and meet people who humbled us because of their humility. We have received the wealth of God's love through His people over and over.

We can also look back and thank our loving God for allowing us to hit bottom in our lives and in our marriage, in order to have our eyes opened to His loving arms and His forgiveness of sins.

The Bible verse quoted above from John 10:10 begins with the words: "The thief comes only to steal and kill and destroy." At different times God has allowed us to have to face "the thief" in order for us to learn to let go and release something. Many times this meant taking the "I" or the "mine" out of our lives or out of the ministry.

To be honest, there were times when we wanted to look back and say, "Did we do the right thing?" Sometimes we wonder, "What would we have done with the land, had the Lord not knocked on the doors of our hearts to release it as well as our lives?"

All we have to do is step outside during a wonderful winter day and hear the laughter of children. All we have to do is see their little

233

bodies stuffed into their snowsuits, riding on one of those big tubes, going down the tubing hill, and screaming all the way. Or recall the heightened noise level of excitement as the tie-breaking point is made in the water polo tournament during the Thursday night overnight at summer camp. Or hear the beautiful voices as our campers sing "How Great is Our God" at closing ceremonies on Friday afternoons. We have been blessed indeed!

A glance to the west out of our kitchen window reminds us that there was once an old grown-up red raspberry patch. But now it is a parking lot jammed full of cars and vans of families ready to hit the hill in the winter or bring their children to camp in the summer or bring a bus load of students for a day on the MAX course.

We can quietly step into great, great grandpa's 1840 barn and see tables full of families enjoying the atmosphere of the ancient beams and the rugged architecture that entices the feeling of yesteryear. We are reminded that this old barn once housed thirteen kittens in the loft over what is now the snack shop. I can close my eyes and envision the ladder that our children used to climb to get to the loft.

Now as we enter into the barn, we breathe in the aromas of pizza, popcorn, and hot chocolate from the snack shop where at one time there was the box stall that housed all kinds of farm animals; especially our children's ponies Fanny and Little Red. One summer staff person, who has been to Five Pines camp all his life, mentioned to me that the "ole barn" (Activity Center) was his most favorite place in the whole world.

Jim has always cherished the hayrides. Some of his favorite times have been driving his tractor round after round on the wooded trails with loads of happy people, using some of the same trails that our son Kirk, cut through the woods when he was just in high school.

On many autumn nights, you can still find Jim standing at the top of the hill overlooking a group of people enjoying a roaring fire in the fire pit under that big old maple tree in Maple Glen Circle. Thousands of people have sat under that ancient maple tree, which has stood there far longer than Jim can remember. It is also a place where he has seen hundreds of campers profess their faith in Jesus Christ for the first time..

For me, I cherish the wonderment that those sweet faces of our campers have brought to my life, and I hope Five Pines has brought to theirs. Their eagerness to always take off into the woods on some adventure, whether it was being a paleontologist or a prospector headed west to find gold. There have been so many priceless times of trudging through the thirty-plus acres twice a day searching out kingdoms of old with our young campers. As long as the Lord allows me on earth, I will always treasure the times of pretending with the campers in the woods or teaching their nimble fingers the craft of the day in the Craft Cottage.

But best of all are the hugs when one of our young campers has something to share about their new-found relationship with Jesus Christ. It melts your heart, and in my heart I sense this message: *"God is producing fruit, and fruit that will last!"* It is amazing to experience all this fun and at the same time have the opportunity to share God's Word and Jesus as Lord.

On my mirror, I have a statement which so beautifully fits our history in the ministry: *"Have openness to being surprised by God."* We have certainly been surprised by God throughout these thirty-five years.

A paraphrase of Psalm 145 again reminds us to *"extol God's name forever and ever ... that one generation will commend God's works to another and tell of His mighty acts."* May *The Tapestry* be a message to our next generation to "tell of the power of His awesome works, and proclaim His great deeds." That is what this book is about.

One day many years ago, I was asked to speak at a women's luncheon. As I closed in prayer, out of my mouth from nowhere came the words of a song I had learned many, many years before as a child. I was so surprised and almost embarrassed. As I got into my car to leave, I knew where those words came from: that still small Voice reminding me of what I had just shared in my talk.

Now as I sit in my living room finishing this book, God has again brought the words of this hymn to mind. They are words that still challenge me every day:

Take my life and let it be, Consecrated, Lord, to thee.
Take my moments and my days; Let them flow in ceaseless praise,
Let them flow in ceaseless praise.
Take my hands and let them move, At the impulse of thy love.
Take my feet and let them be, Swift and beautiful for thee,
Swift and beautiful for thee.
Take my silver and my gold; Not a mite will I withhold.
Take my intellect and use, Every power Thou shalt choose,
Every power Thou shalt choose.
Take my will and make it thine; It shall be no longer mine.
Take my heart, it is thine own; It shall be thy royal throne,
It shall be thy royal throne.

Jim and I will take all these memories and lay them at His feet with a deep, ceaseless praise and gratitude in our hearts.

NOTES

PREFACE
1 *Hope for Each Day,* by Billy Graham, © 2002 by Billy Graham. Used by permission. All rights reserved.

CHAPTER 4
1 St. Augustine, quoted in *The Pursuit of God,* A.W. Tozer, (Camp Hill: Christian Publications Inc., 1982); 33.

CHAPTER 5
1 *Through it All,* André Crouch © Copyright 1971, Renewed 1999. Manna Music, Inc./ASCAP (admin. By ClearBox Rights). All rights reserved. Used by permission.
2 Edward Schillebeeckx, *Jesus* (New York: Seabury, 1979); *Christ: The Experience of Jesus as Lord* (New York: Seabury, 1980).

CHAPTER 8
1 John Piper, https://www.hopeingod.org

CHAPTER 20
1 Albert Einstein, http://www.goodreads.com/quotes/987-there-are-only-two-ways-to-live-your-life-one
2 Ibid, http://www.goodreads.com/quotes/556030-imagination-is-more-important-than-knowledge-for-knowledge-is-limited

CHAPTER 21
1 Warren Weirsbe, http://pastors.com/a-4-part-definition-of-ministry/

CHAPTER 28
1 A.W. Tozer, *The Knowledge of the Holy* (New York: HarperCollins Publishers, Inc., 1961)

CHAPTER 30
1 Marcus Aurelius, (quoted in *Life in the Afternoon,* Edward Fischer,)
CHAPTER 32
1 John Piper, *A Godward Life* (Sisters: Multnomah Publishers, Inc., 1997), 18.

Made in the USA
Columbia, SC
07 April 2019